A lively and engaging stroll through some foundations for . . . education more generally, this is the kind of book we need at this time. Drawing on observation, research, personal anecdote, and historical example, the book reads like a conversation among friends over coffee. While linking democracy and literacy, Tom offers us principles to guide the teaching of literacy, and along the way casually teaches us how to write engaging books.

—**PETER JOHNSTON**, author of *Opening Minds*

As an educator and a researcher in the teaching of writing for over three decades, when I started reading this book, I just couldn't stop, as I continued to feel inspired, reinvigorated, and just couldn't wait to get back inside my classroom. I am sure anyone who reads this book would be similarly inspired and energized to teach and learn.

—**DANLING FU**, author of *"My Trouble Is My English"*

Reading *Literacy's Democratic Roots* is like being invited to pull up a chair in Tom's family room while he narrates a fascinating slideshow of the most important, most lasting ELA concepts that promote "access and diversity." It's a family epic—a pedagogical ancestry that reaches into both our roots and our classrooms today. With his trademark storytelling, Tom chronicles where we've been and inspires us to push ever forward in the best interest of all students. This book is both a record and a call to action; I will return to it again and again.

—**REBEKAH O'DELL**, coauthor of *A Teacher's Guide to Mentor Texts, 6–12*

This is not a book: it's a conversation, or a series of conversations, all of them related to the work we do as teachers . . . with every major thinker who has contributed to and shaped how we teach and think about literacy in the last fifty years. It is a conversation with ourselves as much as with our profession as it was, is, and will be in the coming years.

—**JIM BURKE**, author of *The English Teacher's Companion*

When Tom Newkirk writes, I read. In volume after volume he has pushed my thinking, from considering how our minds are made for stories to the impact that embarrassment has on learning. He demonstrates how exclusionary practices, even when performed with good intentions, slam a door in the face of young scholars. Newkirk challenges us to examine our curriculum for areas where exclusive practices are often the norm—recitation, writing, literary interpretation, book selection—and offers alternative methods for opening wide the door of literacy.

—**CAROL JAGO**, author of *The Book in Question*

Imagine a feast of small, delightful plates. Each bite is rich. You linger over its elements: the hint of curry or cinnamon, the surprising zap of red pepper. This is the closest I can come to describing the power of *Literacy's Democratic Roots*. Each chapter schools you in research and the nuances of teaching well. Newkirk is a wise, gentle guide. There is room to think here, to place these ideas against the grain of your own teaching.

—**PENNY KITTLE**, author and writing teacher at Plymouth State University

Reading a new book from Tom Newkirk is like a long-awaited visit from a really smart and great-hearted friend. After reading this book, I am now much smarter about how to create a democratic classroom, teach for democracy, and support students in developing the dispositions of democracy. This book has reminded me why I teach and has already helped me to meet my deepest commitments and hopes for myself, my students, and for all of society.

—**JEFFREY WILHELM,** Distinguished Professor of English Education at Boise State University

Literacy's Democratic Roots solidifies Tom Newkirk's place at the head of the table of today's most influential writers and thinkers about literacy. Grounded in history and democratic tradition, but especially relevant given the current political discourse, Newkirk's eight big ideas will help you to build a more just, equitable, and engaging classroom. This book should be a starting point for anyone interested in meaningful school reform.

—**KELLY GALLAGHER**, author of *Readicide*

As we strive to promote equity and social justice throughout our schools and society, Tom Newkirk's new book offers educators guiding frameworks and creative ways to rethink literacy teaching and learning in schools and classrooms. Creating democratic classroom spaces where students' stories are viewed as valuable sources of knowledge *alongside the writing in the field* challenges traditional hierarchies and what Tom so aptly labels "killer dichotomies," to create spaces where teachers and students are free to co-create knowledge, write on topics important to them, and work toward a more just society.

—**DIANE WAFF**, Professor of Practice, Director, Philadelphia Writing Project, Penn GSE

In this moment of our history and education, Newkirk reminds us of the democratic constitution of the public school experiment: *everyone* can come in. And everyone can and should come to this book to remember and renew, or to discover for the first time, eight transformative ideas for inviting *all* students to become strong readers, writers, and thinkers. He honors these foundational concepts and their creators as well as several brilliant new voices and practices in literacy education in eight essays that journey through impassioned arguments, illustrative stories, and powerful sample activities to use with students.

—**KATHERINE BOMER**, Professor of Practice, College of Education, University of North Texas

As I read through *Literacy's Democratic Roots*, I found myself reminded of the how and why of successful classroom practice: that the classroom must be a place where student voice is encouraged; that we succeed most when we draw from their funds of knowledge; that rigid formulas for writing or school-imposed titles for reading will usually produce the opposite effect we intend; and that, as Tom has suggested before, the importance of story is not to be underestimated. Tom has written something here that can help both the new teacher, who would benefit from this book's guidance and direction, and the veteran teacher, who needs the occasional reminder of the ideas that inform meaningful and democratic classroom practice. The greatest praise I can give the book is this: that somehow, in the summer after a terrible school year, Tom Newkirk has got me looking forward with optimism to this next school year.

—**MARTIN BRANDT**, author of *Between the Commas*

THOMAS NEWKIRK

LITERACY'S DEMOCRATIC ROOTS

A Personal Tour Through 8 Big Ideas

HEINEMANN
Portsmouth, NH

Heinemann
145 Maplewood Avenue, Suite 300
Portsmouth, NH 03801
www.heinemann.com

Offices and agents throughout the world

The author and publisher wish to thank those who have generously given permission to reprint borrowed material:

p. 54: Jane Kenyon, "Let Evening Come" from *Collected Poems*. Copyright © 2005 by The Estate of Jane Kenyon. Reprinted with the permission of The Permissions Company, LLC on behalf of the Graywolf Press, graywolfpress.org.

p. 63: Excerpt from an unpublished personal letter by Maureen Barbieri. Copyright © by Maureen Barbieri. Reprinted by permission of the author.

Acknowledgments for borrowed material continue on page 204.

Library of Congress Cataloging-in-Publication Data
Names: Newkirk, Thomas, author.
Title: Literacy's democratic roots : a personal tour through 8 big ideas / Thomas Newkirk.
Description: Portsmouth, NH : Heinemann, 2023. | Includes bibliographical references and index.
Identifiers: LCCN 2023014471 | ISBN 9780325161150
Subjects: LCSH: Literacy—Philosophy. | Democracy and education.
Classification: LCC LC149 .N498 2023 | DDC 370.11/5—dc23/eng/20230502
LC record available at https://lccn.loc.gov/2023014471

Acquisitions editor: Anita Gildea
Production editor: Victoria Merecki
Cover and interior designer: Monica Ann Cohen
Typesetter: Monica Ann Cohen
Manufacturing: Jaime Spaulding

Printed in the United States of America on acid-free paper

1 2 3 4 5 VP 27 26 25 24 23 PO 4500876742

To the leadership and staff at Heinemann,
past and present, with profound respect for their commitment
to inviting all students into the house of literacy, for their dedication
to teachers, and gratitude for their unfailing generosity
to me throughout my career.

Contents

Acknowledgments

I realize that this is surely the least-read part of any book, usually attended to only by those who might have some claim to be included. So, I'm tempted to steal a move from Randy Bomer and say that if you are reading this, I acknowledge you. We must have connected in some way, and vibrations of influence are there, even though I cannot properly name that influence here.

I'll start with the leaders and senior editors I have worked with at Heinemann, beginning with Philippa Stratton, who inaugurated the literacy series almost fifty years ago. She was followed by a hugely talented group that included Lesa Scott, Mike Gibbons, Toby Gordon (editor extraordinaire), Lisa Luedeke, Scott Mahler, Lois Bridges, Lisa Fowler, Leigh Peake, Maura Sullivan, Brett Whitmarsh, and Roderick Spelman. Vicki Boyd in particular took a special interest in my work that went miles beyond her official duties.

Margaret LaRaia worked as an editor for my three previous books—I so appreciated her engagement with the topics I was writing on. She pushed me not to be cautious and to write the book that needed to be written. Lad Tobin, though not directly involved with this book, has been an extraordinary reader for me. He continually challenged me to explicitly state what I was trying to do—and he had the uncanny ability to show me a better order for chapters. His voice is in my head.

Anita Gildea served as the editor for this book. In any project there are moments of doubt, when you may think you are just stating the obvious. She helped me through these low spots—in addition to providing multiple fine-grain readings as we went along. Not to mention her great sense of humor, which made our Zoom® meetings fun.

I loved working with the team that brought the book to production. Thanks to Monica Cohen for the arresting cover and interior design. To my friend Kim Cahill for developing a marketing plan and advising on the title. To Pam Bachorz, Jessica Simons, and Lynette Winegarner, who handled permissions in this increasingly restrictive legal environment. The range of citations gave them a lot of work. Elizabeth Tripp did a meticulous copyediting review of the manuscript. And thanks to Victoria Merecki and Jaime Spaulding for shepherding the book through production and into publication.

Catrina Swasey deserves her own paragraph. She was in constant contact with me in the last stages of the book, monitoring the permissions process and making sure I provided the information needed. It was exacting, detailed work, which she carried out with patience and precision. In the end I thought we made a good team as we step-by-step worked through all the details. I foresee a great future for her in publishing.

Once again I relied on Tomasen Carey, coordinator of the UNH Learning Through Teaching (LTT) program, who gave two full readings of the developing manuscript. She could really get on my wavelength and understand what I was trying to do—giving me incentive to keep at it. And thanks to Louise Wrobleski and the LTT faculty for their support in the past. I have rehearsed so much of my writing on them in our meetings. Thanks also to my UNH colleague Christina Ortmeier-Hooper for help on the translanguaging chapter. I also benefited from several discussions of *The Great Gatsby* with Sarah Sherman.

Before I selected the eight ideas, I consulted a number of literacy educators: Michael Smith, Peter Johnston, Jeff Wilhelm, Danling Fu, Deborah Brandt, Russel Durst, Katie Wood Ray, Shawna Coppola, Tom Romano, and Jessica Early. They suggested the terms they would choose (and one of them warned me that the whole project was foolhardy). While I'm sure none would totally agree with the final list, I appreciated their help.

In writing the book, I relied on interviews with literacy scholars, teachers, and students: Sondra Perl, Robert Probst, Laura Lavallee, Ginette Rossi, Nancie Atwell, Penny Kittle, Danling Fu, Katie Wood Ray, Peter Elbow, Marley Beltre, Linda Rief, Mark Holt-Shannon, Eve Hodgdon, and Caitlyn Scully. Dennis Magliozzi helped me with the "Multi" chapter. Danling Fu was especially generous in guiding me through the "Translanguaging" chapter. Mike Michaud helped me on the "Story" chapter—and has been a terrific reader for me. Thanks to Jessica Early and Carol Jago for their thoughtful reviews of the prospectus and sample chapters.

On the home front, thanks to my three children—Sarah, Abby, and Andy—each of whom makes a cameo appearance. Once more, big thanks to my wife, Beth, who again endured endless book reports when I emerged from my office at 11:00 each day. She has helped make a life where this writing can happen.

In a way, this book is *about* acknowledgment—recognizing our roots. But I will leave the rest of that recognition to the book itself. To know who you are, you need to know (to acknowledge) where you came from. You need to know who you stand with and what you stand on. For without a sense of history, we can only blow with the wind, bending to whatever is momentarily current. I hope this book helps establish that ground of being.

Introduction

LITERACY AND DEMOCRACY— OR "WHERE I'M FROM"

If you enter almost any public school, you will encounter a range of offices, for administrators, counselors, nurses, custodians, security. But there will be one type of office you will not find—an admissions office, for the simple reason that public schools are open to all. Don't speak English? You're in. Need a wheelchair to move from place to place? You're in. You've suffered from trauma or have a learning disability? You're in. You're a Democrat, a Republican, a Free Stater? Christian, Muslim, agnostic? You're in.

This absence of an admissions office, this open door, is the extraordinary feature of the public school. Its absence symbolizes a promise, or at least an aspiration, to serve the needs of all who enter, to make everyone feel welcome, respected, at home, and successful. That we so often fall short of this ideal does not negate its significance.

The public school, what Horace Mann called the "common school," open to all, is a great democratic ambition, achievement, and challenge. It was a realization of that wonderful expression of John Adams, prominent in the Massachusetts Constitution (and the New Hampshire Constitution, which copied it), commanding that "in all future periods" governments should "cherish" public education (Volinsky 2004, 837). Cherish, hold dear.

When I first played with the idea of writing about big generative ideas, I considered each chapter a separate unit, unconnected thematically. But when I explained the project to others, the question was always "So how are these tied together?" At first, I resisted this expectation. It felt like I was planning a basic dive—say, a one and a half flip—and someone was asking that I add a full twist. But I became convinced there was a thematic connection—to democracy. Hence the current title.

If someone with way too much time on their hands were to do a word search of all I have written, I suspect *democracy* would not appear. It seemed that democracy, or patriotism, or love of country, was always co-opted by the educational right, who cling to test scores (especially when they show decline), "cultural literacy," (white) nationalism, or a sanitized view of our history, and who at some level see diversity as a problem. Whatever the question, the answer was often testing, standardization, or privatization.

It seemed that democracy, or patriotism, or love of country, was always co-opted by the educational right, who cling to test scores (especially when they show decline), "cultural literacy," (white) nationalism, or a sanitized view of our history and who at some level see diversity as a problem.

A case in point: In 1983, *A Nation at Risk* warned us (melo)dramatically that public education was so deficient that "the educational foundations of our society are presently being eroded by a rising tide of mediocrity that threaten our very future as a Nation and a people" (National Commission on Excellence in Education, 6). Or worse. "If an unfriendly foreign power had attempted to impose on America the mediocre educational performance that exists today, we might well have viewed it as an act of war" (6).

Only one problem—even as the ink was drying from that report, the United States was entering a prolonged period of extraordinary growth, running to about the year 2000, averaging 3.5 percent growth over that period (Macrotrends 2010–23), outpacing the Japanese economy, which was the concern at the time. Clearly US workers, educated in US schools, had something to do with that. Talk about bad predictions. Yet I'm not aware of any retractions or corrections—because only negative national education stories sell.

It has also felt to me presumptuous to justify or explain my ideas in such broad political terms. My focus was usually on the individual student, held back by the constraints of curricula. The title of my last book, *Writing Unbound*, surely emphasized that theme. But as I thought about what the eight ideas in this book have in common, I did feel that there were democratic values at the heart—that they all had to do with access and diversity, with finding ways of connecting educational goals with the funds of knowledge students bring in when they walk through that door.

As I was refining my idea of the book, I sent out a tweet that received a strong response—with some followers turning it into a visual. I wrote: "The house of literacy has a thousand doors. Our job is to help students find one that will let them in." It seemed to me there was the germ of a political idea here—that too many students never entered the house of literacy, and why was that? And what could we do about it? How can we make entry more possible, more inviting, more pleasurable? How are we as educators being held back by rigid ideas and curricula that do not reflect and honor what students, particularly students of color, students outside the mainstream, bring to schooling? How can we disrupt those patterns? How can we tell a better story about literacy? I found that these questions guided me to the ideas I would write about—and that it no longer seemed presumptuous to see this as a democratic issue.

The house of literacy has a thousand doors. Our job is to help students find one that will let them in.

DEMOCRATIC LINEAGES

I take the term *lineage* from the great African American reading specialist Alfred Tatum. He uses the term to describe the reading histories he wants students to develop. Key books in this lineage, ones that speak to their identity, experiences, and aspirations, create a sense of personal tradition—a team, if you will, that supports them and motivates them to read further. He quotes Carl Upchurch, a onetime gang member and convict who went on to become an activist for social justice. A turning point for him was when he came upon a copy of Shakespeare's sonnets, holding up the leg of a wobbly table:

> The literature taught me to look at myself. It told me that regardless of my condition, regardless of the circumstances I came from, I was a legitimate human being and a child of God. (Upchurch 1996, 92)

This concept has special power for those like Upchurch, facing racial prejudice and incarceration. But there is value for all of us, I think, in seeing ourselves as part of an enabling history. It can be extended to family histories, company histories, institutional histories, town histories; to know who you are, you need to know where you come from.

We use quotation to establish this lineage, to place ourselves in a tradition. Too often we teach quotation in a defensive way: we need support for our ideas. It's odd in a way—if we say something, it is suspect but if someone famous said it, then it must be true. I think something far more positive and affirming goes on when we quote from the distant mentors who helped shape our outlook, who, in a sense, helped make us. There are some quotations so foundational for me that I have to hold back on quoting them in everything I write. Here's an example. The great French essayist Montaigne quoted just about every major (and minor) Latin writer. Some of these words he had engraved on the beams of his study. In his essays he defends borrowing this way:

> Bees ransack flowers here and flowers there; but then they make their own honey, which is entirely theirs and no longer thyme or marjoram. Similarly the boy will transform his borrowings so the end-product is entirely his. (1987, 171)

He is arguing that our sources can become so internalized, so much a part of our thinking and worldview, that they are *ours*. In one short metaphor, we have the core of a learning theory. And—appropriately—he lifted this metaphor from his great mentor, the Roman essayist Seneca. He quotes to justify quoting. So it passes from Seneca, to Montaigne, to me, and now to you.

There is another wonderful tradition of quotation—one that seems counterintuitive to beginning writers. We use the present tense: Montaigne *defends*, not *defended*. Even though he wrote those words 450 years ago, and Montaigne the person is long dead, his words are still alive, in the present tense, as we quote them.

DEWEY AND EXPERIENCE

So how might we view literacy practices, the eight ideas of this book, as part of a democratic tradition? What is our lineage? What is the historical tradition we carry on? To draw all the arrows of influence would be too big a task for this writer and for the endurance of the reader as well. But I will briefly suggest two great traditions we draw from. One is the progressive movement in the first half of the twentieth century.

The noted social historian Robert Putnam (2020) credits progressive reforms with what he calls "the upswing" in social well-being. Using an amazing array of statistical measures, he shows how progressive changes expanded education, increased voting rights, strengthened unions, reduced poverty, decreased income disparity, began challenging racism, and helped create communitarian values (which, he documents, are now seriously in decline). In this half century, schools were transformed (Cremin 1961). Public education expanded to include contemporary literature, elective systems, vocational education, reading specialists, counseling services, school libraries, cafeterias, laboratories, and extracurricular sports and clubs. My dad remembers the novelty of high school marching bands around 1930.

One of the major early reformers Putnam cites is Jane Addams, who established a settlement house in Chicago with classes and support for the newly arrived immigrants there. Addams argues that these immigrants brought a rich culture to her city, but one that was neglected (or dismissed) by the schools:

> We send young people to Europe to see Italy, but we do not utilize Italy when it lies about the schoolhouse. If the body of teachers in our great cities could take hold of the immigrant colonies, could bring out of them their handicrafts and occupations, their traditions, their folk songs and folk lore, the beautiful stories which every immigrant colony is ready to tell and translate; could get the children to bring these things into school as the material from which culture

> is made and the material upon which culture is based, they would discover that by comparison that which they [teachers] give them now is a poor meretricious and vulgar thing. (1908, 101–102)

An obvious thread connects Addams' valuation of immigrant Italian culture with, ninety years later, Luis Moll's influential concept of funds of knowledge. There is an even more direct historical connection of Addams to John Dewey, who was a regular visitor to Hull House (they both later helped establish the ACLU). Addams' educational reforms helped shape Dewey's views on education, which he put into practice in his Chicago Laboratory School.

Dewey directly challenged two prevailing conceptions of learning. One was the belief that the goal of education was to create mental discipline, which teachers could develop through a classical education, centered on the learning of ancient languages. What students learned—or how it related to a learner's lived experience—was not particularly relevant. It was the mental work of the learning that mattered. In a perverse way, some argued that the very remoteness, irrelevance, and difficulty of this learning was a virtue—the harder, the better. Dewey and other progressives felt the classical education was too individualistic, too narrow, too unmotivating, too irrelevant to the lived experience of students and the needs of society. Traces of this classical view persisted to my time in high school in the mid-1960s, where the "better" students were channeled into Latin and the "weakest" into Spanish.

Dewey also joined a distinguished set of educational critics throughout history who condemned the focus on the learning of facts or names, purely verbal learning without understanding any concrete experience or thing represented. In *The School and Society*, he makes this ironic comment:

> While I was visiting in the city of Moline a few years ago, the superintendent told me that they found many children each year who were surprised to learn that the Mississippi River in the textbook had anything to do with the stream of water flowing past their homes. (1990, 75)

We can find similar condemnations in Montaigne:

> Our masters stuff these things into our memory, fully feathered, like oracles in which the letters and syllables are the substance of the matter. (1958, 57)

And in Rousseau's *Emile*:

> In any study whatsoever, unless one has the ideas of the things represented, the represented signs are nothing. However, one always limits the child to these signs without ever being able to make him understand any of the things which they represent. (1979, 109)

And in Charles Dickens' devastating portrait of Thomas Gradgrind in *Hard Times*:

> "Now, what I want is, Facts. Teach these boys and girls nothing but Facts. Facts alone are wanted in life. Plant nothing else. And root out everything else." (2003, 9)

The lineage would also include Alfred North Whitehead's (1967) criticism of "inert knowledge": information that we cannot use. And probably the best-known more recent iteration, Paulo Freire's criticism of the "banking concept of education" (1970).

All of this is not to minimize the role of knowledge acquisition, even of facts. One rock-solid foundation in reading research is the central role of "prior knowledge" (Willingham 2006). But we cannot simply, mechanically, deposit ("bank") knowledge in the consciousness of learners, as Gradgrind tried to do. Learners retain information when they see some use for the information, when it helps them solve a problem, make a decision, or even satisfy their curiosity.

Dewey's alternative might be termed "constructivist" or "experimentalist." In fact, he makes good use of the scientific model of experimentation to describe how we think. In effect, *we don't receive knowledge; we make it*. For the process of this making, he uses the term *experience*, easily the most central concept in all his educational writing, and the trickiest.

Experience, as Dewey (1910) conceives it, differs from mere activity, from the daily routines of living, which usually don't require us to think too much. Usually things go as we expect. We turn the key in the lock, and the door opens. But if the door doesn't open, or the key doesn't turn, it sets a chain of experimentation in motion. Are we failing to insert the key properly? We play around with the pressure, maybe jiggling it. Maybe it's touchy. If that doesn't work, we ask, "Is the problem the key or the lock?" And how can we tell? Is it the right key? It may be the right key, but is it defective? Is there another key handy, under some mat or above a doorframe, that we can try? And if that fails too, we might rule out the possibility of a defective key. If it is the lock, has it been changed? Is there a malfunction? Have we noticed problems with it earlier? Is it the bolt or pins in the lock? (And we'll probably need a locksmith if we get this far.)

Intelligence is the capacity to engage in a process and see it through. It also cannot be reduced to following formulas or rigidly adhering to formats or tightly defined rubrics that deprive the learner of agency, creativity, and motivation.

In other words, there is a *process*. There is an arc that begins with the disruption of our routine expectations, leading to possible explanations that need to be tested out as well as, one hopes, a resolution. We open the door. We then bank whatever we learn from the experience, refining our lock knowledge, which we can use in the future.

Teaching is filled with these microexperiments. Literacy educator Cris Tovani tells the story of reviewing standardized test results with a group of teachers. In one case, students in the Denver, Colorado, schools often failed to answer correctly a math story problem that the teachers thought should have been easy for them. It was a simple area problem: students had to calculate the distance a plow must travel to cover an area of field, given the width of a plow row. Cris interviewed students who had trouble with it, asking them to talk their way through it. It turned out that students had trouble visualizing this type of plowing; the kind of plow they knew was a snowplow. Denver and the surrounding area gets so little rainfall (about twelve inches per year) that there aren't farms that would have the kind of cultivation described in the story problem. For these students it wasn't so much a math problem; it was a plow problem.

For Dewey, intelligence is not something you have; it's something you do—also a central tenet of Carol Dweck's concept of the growth mindset (2006). Intelligence is the capacity to engage in a process and see it through. It also cannot be reduced to following formulas or rigidly adhering to formats or tightly defined rubrics that deprive the learner of agency, creativity, and motivation. To engage in a process is to make choices and ultimately to develop a style or a learning identity. Reading specialists Debbie Miller and Emily Callahan (2022), for example, encourage students to complete the stem "I'm the kind of reader who . . ." Or as Peter Johnston (2004) argues, to engage in a process is to tell a story of your learning in which you are the protagonist, even the hero. In effect, Dewey's concept of experience undergirds contemporary formulations of reading and writing as processes, as goal-oriented actions of the learner.

Invisibly, he is everywhere.

Almost from the beginning, Dewey predicted that his conception of education would be misunderstood, and in the 1930s he devoted an entire book, *Experience and Education* (1938), to correcting misconceptions. It is conceptually easier to think in either-or terms—to focus exclusively on the curriculum or on the child rather than on how they interact. Like Addams, he was sharply critical of the isolation of the school from the lived experience of students outside the school:

> From the standpoint of the child, the great waste in the school comes from his inability to utilize the experiences he gets outside the school in any complete and free way within the school itself; while on the other hand, he is unable to apply in daily life what he is learning at school. That is the isolation of school—its isolation from life. (1900/1956, 75)

Yet, later in his career he was equally critical of the other extreme, sometimes called student-centered: viewing the children as capable of determining their own learning path, with the teacher a relatively passive facilitator. This extreme minimized the role of the school and the teacher in helping the student make choices—for to make a choice, you need to be aware of options. Creating that awareness (e.g., through studying mentor texts) is a deliberate process. And those choices need to be part of organized, purpose-driven activity, not just a fleeting preference. They need to be part of a process. Schools should know and draw on the passions, interests, and knowledge of students—developed outside of school—but extend and use them to accomplish school goals. Literacy researcher Anne Haas Dyson has called this the "permeable curriculum" (1993, 217), open to the diverse knowledge, loyalties, and "social worlds" that children bring to and share in school.

THE INTEGRITY OF TEACHER KNOWLEDGE

The other powerful tradition these eight ideas rest on is American pragmatism, also associated with Dewey as well as the Metaphysical Club, an actual group that met regularly in Cambridge, Massachusetts, in the 1870s and included Charles Peirce, William James, and Oliver Wendell Holmes. Collectively they established a distinctively American intellectual tradition that, in the words of Louis Menand, "changed the way Americans thought—and continue to think—about education, democracy, liberty, justice, and tolerance" (2001, xi).

What held this group together was a skepticism about the value of abstractions or ideas perceived as eternal, timeless, immutable—not subject to any practical test. Ideas had to do work, or as William James put it, they had to have "cash value." By that he meant they had to operate in the realm of human experience, solving problems, promoting happiness, helping us make sense of the flux of activity. When they ceased to be of use, they ceased to be true. Menand summarizes the central tenets of pragmatism this way:

> They all believed that ideas are not "out there" waiting to be discovered, but are tools—like forks and knives and microchips—that people devise to cope with the world in which they find themselves. (2001, xi)

And because ideas are created to deal with particular and "unreproducible" situations, they are not permanent but must be revised and adapted (or abandoned) as circumstances change.

Obviously, this view argues that to grow, we must be open to the novelty of new situations and not be locked into routines or preconceptions. Teaching is profoundly situational—and every situation is unique in some way. It is a stunning fact that if we take one sentence from an unpublished piece of writing and put it in a search engine, we won't find a match—*because it has never been written before*. We may have seen similar sentences, similar topics, but that precise paper, even that sentence, is a new event in human history, "unreproducible" in Menand's terms.

It follows that no program, no rubric, no instrument, no checklist, no research result can fully prepare any of us for dealing with novelty. Whatever theories, or research findings, or prescribed questions we have when we enter a class, we must constantly read the situation and improvise—which was never truer than in the pandemic. Any mandate that removes this agency from teachers undermines what we do. Teachers lacking agency can hardly promote agency in students.

Any mandate that removes this agency from teachers undermines what we do. Teachers lacking agency can hardly promote agency in students.

I take another major implication from my reading of the pragmatists, which I call the inductive principle—namely, that we should derive the "rules" we use to guide our practice (teaching, reading, writing, living), not simply receive them. In the area of writing, students are so often bombarded with rules, prohibitions, formats, required structures, and rubrics—passed on from . . . somewhere. There is a heavy deductive, rule-driven, top-down tradition that, in my view, has made writing unappealing.

It's time to say, "Says who?" and to *derive* principles from our reading, our writing, the testimonies of actual practitioners, and mentor texts, to go bottom up. These principles will hardly be uniform and can provide multiple pathways and choices from which we can craft ways of reading and writing that seem to fit us.

If we operate inductively, we discover that many of the "types" of writing we teach are really mixtures, what Gloria Anzaldúa calls "mestiza," from the Latin *mixticius*. It is so easy to accept divisions, what composition scholar Ann Berthoff has termed "killer dichotomies." We create classifications and fool ourselves that they truly represent distinct differences. All category systems leak, and the real interesting work of literacy is exploring how two seemingly different types (genres, media, registers of language, school and home knowledge, the high and the low) mix and interact. One of the most pernicious killer dichotomies is the one that separates the personal and the academic. We also do a disservice when we treat narrative as a separate kind of writing, distinct from argument and exposition—when, in fact, stories are threaded through all kinds of writing. I even argue that to sustain a reader, all writing needs some kind of narrative arc, some plot, some movement from tension to resolution.

There may be another gift we can receive from the pragmatists: optimism. It's in short supply now. And this optimism, this sense of possibility, comes from the focus on the small, the particular. I'd like to illustrate with one more story or parable. When I was a lifeguard at the Ashland, Ohio, public pool, another guard, Bob Doerrer, would often take bets from kids that he could swim the entire fifty-five-yard pool underwater. Nothing big—pennies, a couple of nickels. And he would always win the bet. One day, I decided to try (without the bets) and I asked him if he had any advice. "Just one thing," he said. "Don't look at the end of the pool; keep your focus on the bottom. If you look up, you'll be psyched out."

I dove in and did as he said. I locked my neck so that I could only see the bottom of the pool as I moved along with my breaststroke. Near the end, my lungs burned, and I began to see spots, but I made it (and never tried it again). I took away a moral from this swim: that to do something challenging, you have to focus on the immediate—the small, incremental progress you can make. Forget the big picture. Don't look at the end of the pool.

So I was heartened when I came across a quotation from William James that eloquently captured this idea. It's taken from a letter he wrote in 1899:

> I am against bigness and greatness in all their forms, and with the invisible molecular moral forces that work from individual to individual, stealing in through the crannies of the world like so many rootlets, or like the capillary oozing of water. (in Menand 2001, 372)

I am convinced this attention to the particular, to the moment, to the situation, has both educational value and value for our own well-being. In these situations—each unique in its own way—we make microexperiments, develop microtheories. Not the kind that fill journals, but theories of this child, this day, this moment, this task. We act, observe, evaluate, adjust.

My colleague Les Fisher, a legendary teacher of American literature at the University of New Hampshire, put it more directly. At times when things were discouraging in our department or college, he would hold up whatever text he was teaching—William Carlos Williams, Toni Morrison, Ralph Ellison—and repeat: "It's the work. It's the work."

THE TOUR GUIDE

As I wrote this book, I came to see myself as a tour guide, taking you and other readers through eight big, amazing houses—each with more rooms than we could get to. I have spent time in the rooms of these houses. I've lived in them, and I know others who have helped build and furnish them, even some who set down the foundations. We'll hear from some of them. I will call attention to artifacts in these rooms and tell stories. I'll have to leave out a lot since our time is limited, and almost anyone who has written on literacy in the past thirty years has spent time in these houses or added their personal contribution, even done some of the major (re)construction.

And, while I'm in the mood to admit limitations, let me say that there are other houses of literacy that could have been on this tour. In preparation for writing, I asked a number of scholars what their eight great ideas would be. Many of their suggestions would have made for possible chapters—scaffolding, writing across the curriculum, zone of proximal development, prior knowledge, comprehension strategies, voice, choice, flow, approximation, and metacognition, to name a few. Some of my correspondents tactfully pointed out that the idea of *idea* was vague and that it might include practices, concepts, or fully developed theories. One might protest that independent reading is a practice while Rosenblatt's transactional model of reading is a fully developed theory. To this imprecision, I can only plead guilty.

It is sinful to make students feel inadequate or out of place—to silence them, to treat them as empty vessels, or to make literacy such a chore that they choose not to try. Sinful.

Like most analogies, my metaphor of houses ultimately breaks down because there is considerable overlap in the ideas. Funds of knowledge, for example, kept reappearing in multiple chapters—and I consider it a democratic touchstone, this assertion that students, *all students*, come through the school doors funded, *rich* in personal, family, and cultural knowledge that we need to recognize and use. This premise is central to the role of choice in the writing process, independent reading, and the transactional model of reading as well as other chapter topics.

As I challenged myself to think of a unifying principle for the book, it came down to a core belief that as humans we have the great gift, the great evolutionary achievement, of speech and story. It's what we do best—and all literacy instruction needs to honor and build on that gift. It is sinful to make students feel inadequate or out of place—to silence them, to treat them as empty vessels, or to make literacy such a chore that they choose not to try. Sinful. The traditions of writing instruction in particular—their obsession with form and correctness—need to be corrected.

These eight big *democratic* ideas can help us build a house that everyone can enter.

Chapter One

EXPRESSIVE LANGUAGE

Expressive Language: "It is a verbalization of the speaker's immediate preoccupations and his mood of the moment. . . . It is utterance at its most relaxed and intimate, as free as possible from outside demands, whether those of a task or an audience" (Britton et al. 1975, 82). More often called *talk* rather than *speech*, expressive language is the matrix, the starting point, for more formal and audience-oriented writing and speaking. As James Britton was fond of saying, "talk is the sea upon which everything else floats." Expressive writing has these talk-like qualities, and it is critical for the exploration of a topic. Fluency in writing depends on the writer entering into dialogue with the evolving text—being open to surprise and not being bound by preplanning.

It is tempting to view speech and print literacy as separate human systems, distinct language arts. Oral language—talk and listening comprehension—is innate. We are biologically predisposed to learn it. We accomplish this mastery with lightning speed in childhood. The print counterparts—writing and reading—are not innate; they are learned. Print is too recent an evolutionary development for humans to automatically have mastery over it. We need to be taught to read and write. Writing in particular often feels slow, awkward, and uncomfortably revealing, compared with talk. Mina Shaughnessy has elegantly put it this way:

> The spoken language, looping back and forth between speakers, offering chances for groping and backing up and even hiding, leaving room for the language of hands and faces, of pitches and pauses, is generous and inviting. Next to this rich orchestration, writing is but a line that moves haltingly across the page, exposing as it goes all that the writer doesn't know, then passing into the hands of a stranger who reads it with lawyerly eyes, searching for flaws. (1977, 7)

Consequently, many people, even those with extensive educations, frequently dislike writing, find it laborious, and feel they are not good at it. Most readers find their way to fluency and pleasure, at least in some literary formats, but writing, sadly, is a different story. The key teaching question, a perennial one, is How can we break down this barrier between talk and writing? How can we access our natural expressive capabilities, our ease of expression, when we write? How can we tell a better story about writing?

One way of addressing these questions is to ask, What are the conditions of oral fluency—and how can we translate them to writing? So imagine you are going to see a friend after a long, pandemic-length absence. One thing you are probably not doing is planning what you will say, even though you may be talking throughout the weekend. You don't worry about it. Things will come up; stories will flow—effortlessly.

We are fluent in these occasions because we have an attentive, interested audience, so we can relax. And we come up with things to say because we build off what others say—or what we say. Or even how they lean in and listen. One story prompts another, endlessly, it seems. We often begin speaking not sure where we are going, and the words seem to come. We laugh; humor threads through our talk. We don't take ourselves so seriously that we can't tell a story at our own expense. We don't worry about speaking formally, or making mistakes, or getting off the topic—because there isn't one fixed topic. At its best, we feel as if our whole history, all we have done, read, seen, is available to us—our mind and memory are limber that way.

It is an understatement to say we fail to produce anything near these conditions for fluency when we teach writing in schools.

- The teacher will judge the writing for a grade and note errors. Students will perceive the teacher—the principal reader—as an evaluator.
- The writing must stay on topic; in expository writing, we impose what David Bartholomae has called the "tyranny of the thesis" (1983, 311).
- We overstate the importance of advance planning and fail to disclose the way writers invent as they go.
- We introduce a set of rules and prohibitions that bear no clear relation to what writers actually do.
- We expect a level of formality that is distinct from speech and may even penalize the writer for being too personal. We rarely deal with the importance of humor, particularly in expository writing.
- We treat storytelling as a distinct genre and find no place for it in expository or persuasive writing.

This list could go on. But my point is that traditional writing instruction almost systematically undermines the conditions that make us fluent in oral situations. I'll go even further: we can construct a pretty solid writing approach by inverting all of these practices, turning them on their head and making writing more speechlike.

In *Vernacular Eloquence*, Peter Elbow (2012) makes a powerful case for the primacy of oral language and the ways we can—indeed, must—draw on it when we write. In an interview with me, he put it this way:

> *Our primary relation to language is to speech. Spoken language is in our bones. And I like to use spoken language because it's available to everyone—and the readers, sitting in silence, are likely to hear it in their head. The mouth and the ear are the prime organs of writing.*

He summarized this idea with a favorite slogan: "easy out, easy in."

The stakes are high. Without access to the generative, social, personal characteristics of talk, there can be no fluency, no pleasure, no personal stake in writing. It is a grind—each period becomes a stopping point. Writers who compose this way are called bleeders—it comes drop by drop. In this chapter we will explore ways to rectify this situation and tell a better story about writing by showing its dependence on talk.

WEAVING SPEECH INTO WRITING

Let's start with the lie that there *is* such a unified thing called formal writing. If we look closely, even serious exposition is a weave of written and oral elements. We have a word for language that has only one tone: *monotonous*. A starting point can be the great, great opening to *Moby Dick*:

> Call me Ishmael. Some years ago—never mind how long precisely—having little or no money in my purse, and nothing to particularly interest me on shore, I thought I would sail about a little and see the watery part of the world. (Melville 2018, 13)

The "never mind how long precisely" is a speechlike interjection, almost an irritated response to what he imagines is a question the reader might have, and not an unreasonable one. After all, was this a long time ago or recently? Were you a young man or older? The narrator swats away this question as irrelevant to the story and maybe also as a warning to stop interrupting. "Sit back and listen," he seems to say, "I'll tell you what you need to know." To signal this interjection, Melville uses a dash, an undertaught but dynamic punctuation mark that gives all kinds of freedom to the writer. I am personally addicted to them, like peanut butter cups, and have to ration myself to no more than one pair per paragraph.

According to Peter Elbow, even serious argument and commentary swerves into colloquial speech, and among the examples he includes in *Vernacular Eloquence* is this one from Nobel Prize–winning columnist Paul Krugman, where he describes money:

> Currency—pieces of green paper with pictures of dead presidents on them—is money, and so are bank deposits on which you can write checks. (2012, 349)

Elbow comments:

> I love Krugman's sentence. I think it's good *because* he exploits some of the interesting resources of casual speech. He's enjoying the way spoken syntax interrupts itself, and how it revels in blunt, concrete low-register language. (2012, 349)

It also allows for intimacy and humor, which leaven even serious arguments like the one Krugman is making.

I suppose at some level, I knew that skilled writers did this, but after reading *Vernacular Eloquence* I found it everywhere. For example, take this opening to a *New Yorker* "Talk of the Town" comment on the destructive recall process underway in California:

> September 14 brings the spectre of California's second gubernatorial recall election, and the man in the barrel this time is Gavin Newsom, elected three short years (OK, long years) ago. (Heller 2021, 13)

Heller uses the parenthesis to insert an oral comment as a self-correction, indicating that he had fallen into a cliché ("three short years"). Since these years coincided with the COVID epidemic, they were hardly short. Now, he could have avoided all this by just saying neutrally "elected three years ago," but how much fun would that have been?

The parenthesis is another addictive tool, like the dash. In his short comment piece, Heller uses four, in addition to four pairs of dashes, so I suspect he has to ration himself as well. One thing the parenthesis does is allow a kind of aside, or wink, or personal gesture toward the audience, which can be a tool for humor.

Some might argue that this is all too sophisticated for younger writers, or that "they-need-to-know-the-rules-before-they-break-them."

But in my experience, young writers get this principle. Even before they write on lined paper, young writers show oral emphasis, making some loud words huge. And once they learn exclamation marks, they use them everywhere, often in clusters. Similarly, when they learn to introduce dialogue into their writing, they overdo it. In fact, one of the best early strategies for teaching writing is to show how speech bubbles can work on their drawings.

I suppose it might also be argued that we don't want young writers taking the liberties that these established writers take—especially in expository or argumentative writing. The Common Core State Standards, for example, require a consistent level of academic formality. But why should we expect young writers to be more formal than Paul Krugman?

We need to look at what writers *actually do* and derive principles (but not hard-and-fast rules) from this observation. Writers routinely "violate" just about every rule we set before students.

Elbow's observations about the use of speech features in writing are a good example of the inductive approach to teaching writing—a concept so important it deserves a chapter in itself. To put it simply, usage is king (or queen). We need to look at what writers *actually do* and derive principles (but not hard-and-fast rules) from this observation. Writers routinely "violate" just about every rule we set before students. The test of any experiment or seeming deviation is whether it makes sense in context.

As an example, years ago I was writing an article for *Research in the Teaching of English*, easily the most technical and formal journal published by the National Council of Teachers of English. Even inductively, one could derive the rule that storytelling (and humor), or even the use of *I*, had no place in the established format. I was trying to make the point that in any social situation, we maintain what Erving Goffman calls a "front," a role. And we want to avoid any "discrepant information" that would discredit this role.

I decided to introduce this concept with a story my brother told about his surgery residency. He is left-handed, and much of the setup for surgery assumes right-handedness. This caused him to make some mistakes, and when he made them, he said, "Oops." This went on for a little while, until the head surgeon turned to him and said, "Mr. Newkirk, surgeons do not say 'Oops.'" It seemed the perfect anecdote. And it stayed in, despite the objections of one reviewer.

SELF-PROMPTING

Let's return to the second sentence of *Moby Dick*:

> Some years ago—never mind how long precisely—having little or no money in my purse, and nothing to particularly interest me on shore, I thought I would sail about a little and see the watery part of the world. (Melville 2018, 13)

The "never mind how long precisely" seems a response to a possible question the reader or listener might have. It is as if "Some" prompts the question (Well, how long ago?), which the narrator swats aside. Some kind of dialogue is going on.

We become fluent in writing when we can create a dialogue with the text that is emerging. We need to create the conditions of talk where we are prompted by a listener (*um, um, "What happened next?"* or *"That must have been scary!"*)—and by our own language. We may say a word, maybe the name of our hometown (Ashland, Ohio), and that name opens up for us a constellation of images and memories. The Russian psychologist Lev Vygotsky claimed that some words seem "saturated" with meaning (1962, 148) and our fluency in speaking (and I would add writing) comes from being alert to that saturation, that suggestiveness, which can take us in directions that we hadn't planned for. While I can't vouch for Melville's thought process, I would bet that he *hadn't thought* of his famous interjection until he wrote, "Some years ago." That was the trigger.

My mentor Donald Murray described this suggestive process as "listening to writing." The emerging text, for him, takes on a life of its own, directing the writer in the next steps:

> Neither published writers nor beginning students have much control over what a piece of writing is going to say as it is talking its way toward meaning. Both must listen to the writing to hear where it is going with the same anticipation and excitement we feel when a master story teller spins out a tale. (1982, 63)

I'll admit that when I first read this, it felt way too mystical for me—the text taking control, telling the writer what to do. Surely the writer, not the inanimate text, is making the decisions. In retrospect, I was taking Don too literally. I now feel he was describing the sensation of being caught up in the act of creation, something psychologists would later call flow. It is not a passive situation, but it is also not one where the writer is exercising tight control. It is a flexible mindset, responsive to opportunities and accidents, even if that means deviating from a plan. In jazz it might be called improvisation.

After all, no matter how carefully we plan, we cannot anticipate every word we will write and say—there are bound to be surprises and unexpected opportunities. Put another way, there are progressive expectations—that things will move forward in a logical way. And there are digressive possibilities, side adventures, new possibilities, maybe better possibilities, that occur during the writing. We can move forward or sideways—and our schooling is biased in favor of forward. But if we aren't open to the unexpected opportunities that writing presents, our writing tends to be thin, skeletal, and so unidirectional that the reader feels pushed around. (Virginia Woolf [1989] mocked this kind of linear thinking in *To the Lighthouse.*) There is a lack of exploration and variety. To be sure, writing that is *overly* digressive is also frustrating, though digression is celebrated in *Tristram Shandy* (Sterne 2003), where the narrator constantly gets distracted and can't make it to his own birth.

A major barrier to lateral movement is our concept of topic, or what it means to stay on topic. In essay writing, as it is usually taught, the topic is constrained by a thesis that sharply limits what can be included. David Bartholomae offers this criticism of the way we often teach the thesis:

> In assignment after assignment, we find students asked to reduce a novel, poem, or their own experience into a single sentence, and then to use the act of writing in order to defend or "support" that single sentence. Writing is used to close a subject down, rather than open it up, to put an end to discourse rather than open up a project. (1983, 311)

Eighth grader Caitlyn, an avid fiction writer, gave a similar response when I asked her what advice she would give to writing teachers:

> *Don't tell kids what to write—let them figure it out for themselves. You can give them maybe a sentence or two to start them off—maybe a word to start off. But don't make them base it on one thing. Let them expand and go where they want to be. Don't keep them on the railroad track—go off the tracks.*

I asked her what kind of "railroad tracks" limited students. She mentioned being required to use certain words or strict rules about staying on a topic:

> *If you are writing about an apple, you could not write about a pear or a banana—it has to be about the apple.*

But how, exactly, do we go off the tracks?

What Murray calls listening to the text is not some mystical process; it is something we do all the time. Language prompts more language. Within the sentence, the subject (Rafael Devers) prompts the verb (homered), and the verb prompts elaboration (in the ninth, completing a great comeback for the Boston Red Sox®). Technically, this is the enormously useful, right-branching cumulative sentence, first championed in the 1960s by Francis Christensen. Interestingly, he called the process "generative" since the opening to the sentence triggers the elaboration to come later (i.e., to the right). Whenever we get in a tangled, complex sentence, it's useful to get the subject and verb first and go from there.

James Britton (1982) described this process as "shaping at the point of utterance," arguing that writers can adapt the inventiveness and spontaneity of speech in their writing: "Once a writer's words appear on the page, I believe they act primarily as a stimulus to *continuing*—to further writing" (140). Peter Elbow made exactly the same point in our interview. His famous nonstop freewriting exercises push writers to abandon conscious planning and formal language—they must rely on what he calls the "vernacular."

> *Unplanned language coming out of the mouth is highly shaped. It conforms to the grammar of the native speaker. Once you can stop planning and get to the vernacular language, that's better.*

The language is better, he claims, because it is more concrete, more comprehensible, a language of the people, "of the earth."

In a similar way, sentences can prompt subsequent sentences if we are responsive to the emerging text, to what is happening before us. These connections are sometimes called moves, which I would define as a shift in thought, as if the writer is responding to a question the reader might have. I would argue that they are far more important than organization that comes from advance planning. Fluency is the capacity to make moves, usually instinctively, but with even a bit of reflection, we can come up with a good list of moves writers make.

Here is my list, the questions ever-present as I write:

What is this about?

What do I really want to say?

What happens next?

What does it look like, feel like, smell like?

Why is it important?

What does it resemble?

What's my reaction to it?

What example or experience can I use to clarify it?

How does it connect to other reading I have done?

Who would disagree with it and why? What would I say back?

What do I mean by it?

How could I restate it?

These are my chess moves, recurring invitations to expand. I sometimes feel like there is a lighthouse beacon in my brain that is scanning all I have done, read, and seen, searching for connections, mining for material that is relevant to the writing.

And how do writers internalize these moves? From reading in the genres they are writing in (particularly close reading as a writer) and from hearing these questions from readers of their own writing. But mostly from really attending to the text they are creating, listening to the text. Obviously one problem is that we ask students to write in genres—particularly literary analysis—that they don't read, and so they lack the opportunity to see the key moves of those genres.

I can't fully describe it, but there are a few features of this process that are important for me:

- It has been helpful for me to see my autobiography as a series of informative anecdotes that I can call on when useful (the story of my surgeon brother, for example). I have never felt I had a grand narrative to relate, but I hoard moments that have taught me something. It is a serious, serious mistake to think that these moments are too personal or anecdotal.
- I try to be tolerant of digressions that seem to take me offtrack. Sometimes I end up deleting them, but often the digressions are better than what I had planned to write.
- Of all these prompts, the most important one has to do with imagining legitimate and thoughtful resistance to what you have written—and to treat that resistance respectfully. One of my colleagues has called this "counterdiscourse." Not only does this add dynamism and conflict to the writing, but it also demonstrates a mindset that is not dogmatic and absolute, but rather pluralistic and welcoming of serious debate. Beginning writers sometimes feel that opposition weakens their argument, when the opposite is true.
- The more we use these prompts as a scanning device, the better and more automatic it becomes. The more we write, the more these channels open up. In a reversal of physics, the more we pour from the beaker, the fuller it becomes.
- Digression favors the prepared mind—you have to digress to *something*, and the fuller your background in the topic, the

I sometimes feel like there is a lighthouse beacon in my brain that is scanning all I have done, read, and seen, searching for connections, mining for material that is relevant to the writing.

> more places you have to go (another problem, I think, with the literary analysis paper).

FREEWRITING

Some form of freewriting is part of the repertoire of most writing teachers I know. Its most influential champion is Peter Elbow, who in *Writing Without Teachers* (1973) argued against a seemingly self-evident idea about control—that we should make decisions in advance of writing, planning, outlining so that we don't get offtrack. It would seem that the advance control can take the pressure off the writer. But Elbow argues the opposite, that it inhibits writers who never gain fluency because this vision of control misconceives the whole process:

> Instead of a two-step transaction of meaning into language, think of writing as an organic, developmental process in which you start writing at the very beginning—before you know your meaning at all—and encourage your words gradually to change and evolve. (15)

The more we write, the more these channels open up. In a reversal of physics, the more we pour from the beaker, the fuller it becomes.

Paradoxically, by suspending the requirement for advance control, and the expectations of the reader, writers are able to get words on paper and discover (as in talk) what they really want to say. Language is able to do what it does best—find more language, find meaning. Writers *control a process* that allows them to produce writing.

Elbow's argument parallels that of Dorothea Brande in her 1934 guide (still in print) *Becoming a Writer*. Brande viewed the unconscious as a far more powerful resource than conscious planning:

> The unconscious should not be thought of as a limbo where vague, cloudy, and amorphous notions swim hazily around. There is every reason to believe, on the contrary, that it is the great home of form; that it is quicker to see types, patterns, and purposes than our intellect ever can be. (151)

Both Brande and Elbow recommend freewriting—writing quickly and continuously for about ten minutes. The goal is to outrun the mental censor, suspend any audience awareness, writing badly to write well. As Elbow says, "let words talk to words." Change subjects if you wish. The goal is productivity. Others call this a quickwrite or word sprint. The writing is colloquial, maybe rambling, talk-like because it is virtually impossible to write formally under these conditions.

Freewriting invitations can be totally open, with no suggested topic, or they can be focused on some kind of prompt. In *The Quickwrite Handbook*, Linda Rief (2018) shows how we can use excerpts from mentor texts to prompt writing. The mentor text can suggest a topic and show a way of writing about it. Early in a writing class I always ask students to write about food; it is a universal topic, and I love reading aloud a section of Charles Simic's essay "Food and Happiness" (1994).

Simic grew up in what used to be Yugoslavia, after World War II when food was scarce. He describes an eating contest with his uncle, "one of those wonders of nature everybody envies, a skinny guy who can eat all day long and never gain weight." They're eating big plates of beans, on an outdoor terrace, with all the neighbors watching. At one point, Simic is so full he slides off his chair onto the floor:

> I'm dying, it occurred to me. My uncle was still wielding his spoon with his face deep in the plate. There was a kind of hush. In the beginning, everyone talked and kidded around, but now my aunt was exhausted and had gone to lie down. There were plenty of beans but I was through. I couldn't move. Finally, even my uncle staggered off to bed, and I was left alone, sitting under the table, the heat intolerable, the sun setting, my mind blurry, thinking, this is how a pig must feel. (8)

A great read-aloud piece.

Sometimes the prompt is a told story. Mark Holt-Shannon, an eighth-grade teacher I have worked with, claims that "to teach story you have to tell stories, just talking and kind of basking in the feeling of a well-told story." When I invited students to write about endlessly retold family stories, I was sure to tell my own about a late-night call from the university campus police.

> The call came at about 3:00 a.m., jarring our sleep. My wife took the call, and I overheard a short conversation, after which she came into the bedroom and said, "There's a UNH police officer in your office and you're to call him." So I dialed my own number and an officer answered quickly.
>
> "Professor Newkirk, I am in your office and it appears to have been ransacked. There is paper strewn on the floor and all over your desk. The lights were on. The door unlocked, window open. File drawers are open." He paused. "But nothing seems stolen—your tape recorder and typewriter are still here."
>
> Then he paused as if understanding something. "Professor Newkirk, I don't mean to be impolite . . . but could you have left it this way?"
>
> I admitted that I probably had left it that way.
>
> "Well," he said, "I'll turn off the lights and lock the door and wish you a good night."

Sometimes I add a double-listing step before the writing. The first list is possible topics—things on your mind, reactions to school, current annoyances, memories, something in the news. Once writers complete this list, I ask them to circle the best possibility for writing, put that topic at the top of the page, and write another list of any details, words, things that connect with that topic. Then we all write, fast, with no stopping to edit.

There are a number of low-risk ways of responding to this freewriting.

- ***The Sweep:*** Go around the class and have each student say in a sentence or two what they have written. In this way I hear something from every student, even the shy ones.
- ***The Chorus:*** Have each student pick a sentence they like. I point to class members, who then read their sentence.

- *Peer Sharing:* In one-on-one pairings, students either read or summarize what they have written.
- *Count the Words:* I have everyone count how many words they've written to show proof that we can be fluent.
- *Locate the Center of Gravity:* I have students look for some key idea, image, surprise, or insight that occurred during the writing. Again, this is a Peter Elbow idea.

The freewriting students do is often looser, just plain better, and more readable than what they do on papers or essays. And, the freewriting helps me know them better, and I can use this knowledge as a resource when we turn to analytic or research writing. A student whose parents bitterly divorced may have opinions about divorce—Luis Moll called this a fund of knowledge the student brings to school. Freewriting helps us tap into that fund of knowledge.

TAKING THE BLANK TURN

Feedback is obviously important for writers, really anyone learning a skill, but as teachers we want that feedback to be useful—to be used. Otherwise we expend energy for no benefit. Traditionally, feedback focused on grading, even correcting, once a student turned a paper in. Needless to say, this expectation to correct all errors made the teaching of writing a miserable form of work, leading one early-twentieth-century teacher to rejoice in being freed from such teaching to exclaim: "I thank God I have been delivered from the bondage of theme work into the glorious liberty of literature" (Carpenter, Baker, and Scott 1903, 329).

> While correcting work may prove the teacher's attentiveness, even rigor, it's quite a stretch to imagine that the recipients of this tedious work actually learn something from it.

And to what end? While correcting work may prove the teacher's attentiveness, even rigor, it's quite a stretch to imagine that the recipients of this tedious work actually learn something from it. It would be necessary that they (a) reviewed the corrections and comments; (b) understood the principles or rules behind the corrections; and (c) transferred the principles of the comments to new writing tasks. It is magical thinking to imagine that this happens very often. Students look at the grade and move on.

Several years ago, I held a series of workshops for faculty in the various disciplines, and I asked them all to make a timeline of a writing assignment, from the creation of the assignment to the point of final evaluations—and I asked them where they spent their time. In most cases it was something like 15 percent in designing and explaining the assignment and almost all of the rest in reading and grading the writing. It was heavily backloaded—almost all the time spent was at the end of the sequence. I invited them to reimagine this pattern, not adding time, but repositioning it, doing more earlier within the process and less later. After all, wouldn't time spent helping the student plan the writing—maybe talking through it—have better odds of success than time spent offering criticism that might (but most likely won't) be used in some future writing?

Feedback is often nondialogic, a one-way communication with the student. We might write on a draft, "Add detail here," but if the student has no sense of what a detail is, or what detail to add, or why detail is needed, it is unlikely they will add it. *Because they need to hear themselves speak*. If, in a conference with the student, I say, "Could you tell me more about *x*?" and if I convey to the student real curiosity and patience, there is a good chance the student will have more to say about *x*. It will activate their memory; they'll recall a detail, like the smell of their father's cigar smoke. Once they've spoken this new detail, we have new possibilities for expansion. It's out there, heard, made possible by the exploratory talk. This process is particularly important for inexperienced writers who regularly underwrite and need tools of expansion.

As writers develop, they internalize many of these prompts, which become part of the unconscious act of composing. As Vygotsky claimed, the interpersonal becomes the intrapersonal (1978, 90). Even young writers sometimes say they can give themselves a writing conference. One invaluable tool is what I have called the blank turn. Normal teacher-student interaction follows a pattern of initiation–response–evaluation (Mehan 2014): the teacher asks a question, the student responds, and the teacher comments on the response. It's the default mode of classroom talk. It is a form of recitation, with the teacher indicating whether the student has given the right answer. We've all been there.

But we can disrupt this pattern by refusing to ask a specific question and inviting the writer to say more about something. "Say more about why this topic interests you." "Say more about this moment in your story when . . ." And then we should do everything we can, eye contact, body language, and so on, to be fully present as a listener, to create an inviting psychological space. When the writer comes to a stopping point, we can refuse to evaluate or even comment—we can take the blank turn and simply invite more talk. "Tell me more." "What else?" Or just a judicious silence. Often we all need more than one try to say what we want to say.

This doesn't—can't—go on forever, but once the student has taken a good long turn, I can summarize or note details and observations that might be useful in a revision or in the next stage of writing. In the best writing conferences, something new or unanticipated is created through talk, mostly student talk. I try to follow an old Shaker motto: never miss an opportunity to keep your mouth shut.

In the best writing conferences, something new or unanticipated is created through talk, mostly student talk. I try to follow an old Shaker motto: never miss an opportunity to keep your mouth shut.

An interaction like this is a model, I feel, for the kind of internal rehearsal writers do all the time. We are modeling an internal listener or prompter that the writer can appropriate and internalize. We *do* hear voices when we write, and they are not always helpful ones: they can try to convince us that our writing is deficient, that we are saying nothing new, that we have no business writing on a topic that others know far more about. Let's call this negativity by its proper name: self-bullying. To be fluent, we need to internalize a more generous audience, a respectful, nonjudgmental, curious reader, one who leans in and invites us to say more.

Since the Middle Ages, inventors have tried to create a machine that once set in motion will not stop, will not run down. Often the machines looked like the image in Figure 1.1 (page 18), a wheel with balls that take advantage of gravitational force. But it can't be done—there cannot be a frictionless machine—and they all run down, as the laws of thermodynamics would predict.

But language, it seems to me, is as close to a perpetual motion machine as we are likely to get. Our brains have astonishing associative power. Language is endlessly generative; words call up words—and what is amazing is that the sentences we write, even pedestrian ones like this

We need to show that writing, fluent writing, is possible when it builds from the foundation of speech, from the moves of conversation that we all intuitively use all the time.

one, have never been written before. This sentence is a new event. Try to find it on Google™.

My dream is helping beginning writers feel that richness, that potentiality. And the way to do that is not to present them with a set of rules or with rubrics that indicate what must be in a type of writing. We need to show that writing, fluent writing, is possible when it builds from the foundation of speech, from the moves of conversation that we all intuitively use all the time. It is entering into dialogue with our own writing, speaking to ourselves, encouraging ourselves. As teachers, we can help create this other self, by modeling it so that students might internalize it. The dream is that long after their time with us is over, our former students can still hear us saying, "You're onto something. Tell me more."

Figure 1.1 *The Perpetual Motion Machine*

Chapter Two

FUNDS OF KNOWLEDGE

Funds of Knowledge: "The historically accumulated and culturally developed bodies of knowledge and skills essential for household or individual help, individual functioning and well-being" (Moll et al. 1992, 133). This term encompasses practical knowledge for, among other things, home repair, cooking, planting, hunting, healing, child-rearing, and entertaining. Originators of the term distinguish it from the more general term "culture," which is often more associated with folklore such as storytelling, crafts, and the arts. They stress that children come to school well stocked with information and interests that we can draw on in school learning.

Let's start with candy. In the early 1990s, an education professor, Luis Moll, and a team of two anthropologists and a classroom teacher set out to document the funds of knowledge in a working-class Tucson, Arizona, community—and to use their findings to make the school curriculum more culturally relevant to students. They trained a group of teachers to visit households and use open-ended ethnographic questioning to learn about the household expertise that they might bring into the classroom. During one of the visits, they noticed sixth grader Carlos selling candy that he had brought in from Mexico, where he spent his summers. Indeed, half of the children in his class regularly traveled to and from Mexico—and Carlos in particular was a real entrepreneur, a participant in international commerce. In another visit, the teachers learned that one of the parents in Carlos' class made and sold *pepitoria*, a Mexican treat, so the teachers decided to use candy as an inquiry theme.

The class generated questions—including What ingredients are used in the production of candy in the United States and Mexico?—and they were surprised to see how many fewer ingredients were in Mexican candy. Mrs. Rodriguez, the candymaking mother, came to class and demonstrated how to make *pepitoria*. While it was cooking, she talked to the class about how to make different kinds of candy, US and Mexican food consumption, and the nutritional value of candies. Once the *pepitoria* was finished, the students packaged, priced, and sold it.

This is a good example of the relationship between spontaneous and scientific concepts (Vygotsky 1962). These border-crossing students had formed their own opinions about their preferences between US and Mexican candies—different levels of sweetness, for example. Teachers built the school-based scientific concepts—scientific method, nutritional

value, artificial versus natural coloring, candy consumption and production—upon the everyday spontaneous concepts that the students brought to the class. These everyday concepts bring life and relevance to learning—and the scientific concepts help students see these experiences in a systematic way. In other words, schooling is not simply about validating funds of knowledge but about using them.

Let us pause for a moment and appreciate the term *funds of knowledge*. *Funds* implies wealth, a deep reservoir of resources to draw on and spend—implicitly refuting the pervasive deficit models that have minimized what students of color bring to schooling. And *knowledge*—not simply experiences (or culture) but actual knowledge—insights and skills gained through experience that have or should have the same status as any school learning. That is the implicit claim so elegantly put forward in the term.

As already indicated, Moll crafts his pedagogical work on the sociocognitive work of Lev Vygotsky, and one Vygotsky quote is particularly significant:

> That the school has been locked away and walled in as if by a tall fence from life itself has been its greatest failing. Education is just as meaningless outside the real world as is a fire without oxygen, or as is breathing in a vacuum. (in Moll 2014, 121)

In an interview with a high school teacher working in Chandler, Arizona, I got a sense of just how high, how impenetrable, this fence has been. She went to the same high school that Rudolfo Anaya, one of the founders of Chicano literature, had attended—but she never was introduced to his classic *Bless Me, Ultima* until later in college. The same was true for another Phoenix high school teacher whom I interviewed. She was an A student in high school, where she read Shakespeare every year, completely unengaged. "I did the packets." It wasn't until college, when she read Sandra Cisneros and Gloria Anzaldúa, that she found reading addressed to her. A tall fence indeed.

For Vygotsky (and Moll), this outside knowledge is key to engaging children and to making school meaningful. It's the oxygen of learning.

But this outside knowledge interacts (or can interact) with the objectives of school—and it is this meeting, this dialectic, that is central. Schools, for example, can introduce genres, vehicles for students to use and extend their understandings and passions. They can provide a vocabulary to help name some of these experiences and let students see them in a more abstract and systematic way. For example, my friend and reading specialist Ellin Keene insists on teaching young readers what terms like *inference* and *schema* mean.

Critical race theorist Tara Yosso (2005) has created a framework, called "community cultural wealth," that elaborates the resources that children in communities of color can bring to schooling. She identifies six admittedly overlapping forms of "capital":

- ***Aspirational Capital:*** "the ability to maintain hopes and dreams for the future, even in the face of real or perceived barriers" (77)
- ***Linguistic Capital:*** the capacity to use multiple languages and be proficient in recounting stories, parables, and proverbs
- ***Familial Capital:*** "those cultural knowledges nurtured among *familia* (kin) that carry a sense of community, history, memory, and cultural intuition" (79)
- ***Social Capital:*** the ability to use networks of people and community resources
- ***Navigational Capital:*** "the skills of maneuvering through social institutions" (80)
- ***Resistant Capital:*** the persistence to oppose and resist subordination and injustice

The predominant deficit models, in her view, are blind to these forms of capital. There are a number of other important concepts or teaching frames for students of color that overlap with funds of knowledge. Among these are Muhammad's "equity framework for culturally and historically responsive literacy" (2020); Tatum's "textual lineages" (2009);

Germán's "culturally sustaining practices" (2021); and Ladson-Billings' "culturally relevant pedagogy" (1995).

Jessica Lander, a high school civics teacher and author of *Making Americans: Stories of Historic Struggles, New Ideas, and Inspiration in Immigrant Education*, argues that the immigrant experience can be an asset in schools:

> Their journeys to America have often made them masters of negotiation, problem solving, teamwork, and language. For one of my students English is not a second language but his 10th. They develop powerful skills as linguistic and cultural translators for their families, and remarkable perseverance, honed by learning to live in a new land. (2022, A11)

Educators must figure out how to become aware of these strengths and how to leverage them in the curriculum.

WHO ARE YOU?

The concept of funds of knowledge has particular relevance for marginalized groups—Moll focused his own attention on Mexican American students in the Southwest, who were often given low-level tasks to do in school. His associate Cathy Amanti writes:

> The type of educational practice often prescribed for working-class and minoritized students is rote learning in small incremental steps. I find this type of teaching to be stifling and unnecessary. My students are as capable of developing and carrying out their own inquiry-based research projects as students of any background. In addition, when learning incorporates topics central to students' own lives, they become more confident and engaged learners. (2005, 137–38)

This belief in the wealth of knowledge students possess is especially relevant for English language learners, who can practice the craft of invisibility. They may stay silent during class discussions, perhaps embarrassed by their accents or by the times they are asked to repeat themselves when they do try English and are unable to formulate responses on the fly in a fast-moving conversation. If they *are* called on, there is that startled look and defensive minimal response. In other words, a teacher might be tempted to make judgments about verbal ability, even intelligence, based on this silence. It can seem like nothing is there, a deficit to be sure.

But I'd like to argue the concept is profoundly useful for teaching writing to *all* students. If all writing (indeed, all learning) comes from some autobiographical base, it is important for teachers to know some of that autobiography. The more we know, the more effective we will be in engaging students in writing—indeed, in schooling altogether.

Don Graves once posed this challenge: Make three columns. In the first column, list—without checking your roster—all of the students in your class. In the second column, name something that each student knows or can do. In the third column, put a check if the student knows that you know this about them.

When I try this with my college classes, around the second week, there are always two or three students I forget in the first column, often a Jessica or Jennifer who doesn't speak and disappears from my view. The exercise prompts me to see, and get to know, that student.

Learning this information is obviously helpful in developing meaningful writing choices. But on a more fundamental level it provides a point of contact. If, horror of horrors, I find that one of my students is a New York Yankees® fan, we definitely have something to talk about.

I will argue, along with Moll and his colleagues, that we can leverage these competencies and interests to fulfill educational goals—they can be topics for stories and inquiries. But they have importance beyond that. In our classes we see a part of the student, and if we're honest, writing and reading may never be central to their identity—hard as we might try to make it central.

But if we look more widely, we can recognize other skills. A student may be a superb soccer player, or do volunteer work at an animal shelter, or fix cars with their dad, or take care of brothers and sisters. In effect, a student says to us: "I am more than you can see of me in this class." By taking a wide-angle view of students, we can build lasting connections to students who may not have thrived in our classes. We see, for example, that the quiet young girl who rarely speaks in class is a fierce defender on the soccer team, shouting out directions to teammates. That image is important. *There is more to me than you see.*

In effect, a student says to us: "I am more than you can see of me in this class." By taking a wide-angle view of students, we can build lasting connections to students who may not have thrived in our classes.

While few teachers can do the ethnographic surveys that Moll and his associates did, there are, of course, time-honored ways of bringing the outside in. Show-and-tell was first written about in 1954 and was probably around long before that. Home visits are rarer these days, but when my mother taught in a one-room school, she would visit the homes of all of her students, have dinner with them, and often spend the night. Primary-grade teachers meet with their incoming students and pay special attention to the loyalties shown on the T-shirts and sweatshirts they wear (talk about a clue!). Jessica Early, an education professor at Arizona State, participated in writing groups with parents and their teachers—with a lot of the writing in Spanish. And always there is the call of stories.

As I noted in the previous chapter, one opening move in a writing class can be storytelling, specifically family legends. These are the stories, sometimes humorous, or heroic, or instructive, that are told and retold, embellished with each retelling. They are profoundly important; there is even research suggesting that knowing family lore (e.g., the story of the day you were born) is psychologically beneficial. These stories are prominent at the milestone moments of our lives—wedding reception toasts, roasts, retirements, memorial services. A young woman in one of my classes told the story of how she caused two accidents with her boyfriend's car *in the same day* (and he stayed her boyfriend). In my classes I would usually begin by telling one of my stories. The 3:00 a.m. call from the campus police officer was one. Here's another:

> In the mid-1950s the Ohio Turnpike was completed, making our trip to my mom's parents in northwest Ohio so much faster and easier. The turnpike was a new experience for us—one-way traffic, tolls, exits, with service plazas, where we would sometimes eat on the way.
>
> The restaurants were not today's fast-food stops. There were waitresses and tablecloths, and it was not cheap for

> my parents. After one stop, we left the restaurant, and a couple of miles down the road, my dad realized that in the confusion of exiting the restaurant, he had failed to pay the bill. I remember my brother and me immediately looking behind our car to see if we were being trailed by state patrolmen.
>
> My mom sensibly suggested that we just mail the payment when we got to her parents' house. But my dad decided he had to go back to the restaurant—which meant driving to the next exit, paying the toll, getting back on the turnpike heading east, paying the toll at the exit before the restaurant, and getting back on the turnpike heading west until we came to the restaurant, where he paid the bill (they hadn't even noticed he hadn't paid).

I took a moral from this that sounds banal as I write it but is tied, I think, to this episode—when you make a mistake, correct it as soon as possible. That way it doesn't hang over you. It is part of my personal fund.

A Phoenix-area teacher I interviewed described how she tied this storytelling into her unit on heroes:

> *Every unit I plan is based on who my students are as human beings. In the unit on heroes we're reading about the hero's journey, and I try to talk to them about who are the heroes in your life already—and they don't have to be superheroes. And why are they heroes? How are ordinary people heroes in your own story? Everything I do involves students writing about who they are and where they come from and why they make choices based on what they learned from home.*

Some of what they share in class is more everyday, like the "neighborhood walk"—"where they teach me something they have been taught, like a grandmother's story of an old recipe that comes from the family."

Moll advises those interested in seeking out funds of knowledge to "pay attention to detail, for we are interested in the mundane—that which is easy to overlook—in the concrete conditions and practices of life" (2014, 123). That's also good advice for the quickwrites. The mundane—food, hair, pets, siblings, annoyances, small preferences. Montaigne, for example, went on at length about whether he liked drinking from clear or opaque glass containers.

Our best topics are often right in front of us, obvious and unrecognized. For some time, my neighbor and friend Don Murray had a George Booth *New Yorker* cartoon on his bulletin board. It depicts a man seated on his porch before a typewriter, arms folded, obviously experiencing some kind of writer's block. He is surrounded by dogs, by my count about seventeen—all varieties: pit bulls, sheepdogs, a dachshund, a shih tzu, and a Scottie, in addition to a litter of puppies in a cardboard box. A dog peers out at him from a window—and there is a picture of a favorite dog on the wall of the porch.

And still he sits.

His wife stands in the doorway and offers him this advice: "Write about dogs!"

THE THINGS WE CARRY—IDENTITY THEMES

I have borrowed (OK, stolen—I don't remember asking or intending to return) a term from my friend Jeff Wilhelm—"identity theme" (2013)—that has proven useful for me. An identity theme is a foundational character trait or passion that orients us, that defines us, and that we draw on to choose books, to choose topics for writing, or to take stands among conflicting ideas. It is our autobiographical home base; it enables us to have a point of view, an attitude. It may be rooted in family history, in profound losses or challenges or achievements that have shaped our value system. It can be about fears and longings. An identity theme, then, is more deeply rooted than an interest—of which we all have many.

To the extent that we can name and know these themes, we can use them. I am convinced they are the engine that drives us—invaluable for the writing teacher to know. Our goal as writing teachers, I am convinced, is to help students use the tools we teach—particularly the range of genres available—to engage these identity themes. It's an exchange.

The energy comes from this autobiographical base, but we then channel it into forms, such as the podcast, the editorial, the review, and the research essay, that make up our curriculum. We piggyback on these themes.

Ginette Rossi, a sixth-grade teacher in Phoenix, begins her year with an art project in which she invites her students to portray parts of their lives that might be perceived by others as deficits but that are really assets. After they complete the art project, the students write a commentary to explain its significance. Ginette begins the sharing, as she explains:

> *I come from a history. I come from addiction. My mother was a heroin addict and my father was an alcoholic. I tell them that I don't know my birth father—and that resonates with some of them who were adopted and think it's a shameful secret. I tell them about domestic violence in my home growing up. I make sure they know that I am not defined by my past. I also tell them about what I have achieved, about friendships, and my aunt and grandmother, who really raised me. I talk about my love of food—Mexican and Italian culture is similar—food, saints, religion are aligned. So, when I talk about making the ravioli, they understand because they are making tortillas.*

Her sharing opens the door to talk about food and traveling back and forth to Mexico. One student told the story of his grandfather in Mexico who had a passion for Whataburgers, famous in the Southwest, and how desperate he was for them during the pandemic. This talk of food led to a second project, a recipe book with each of her 118 students contributing, a project that often required the translation of an intuitive family practice into clear directions.

I believe that there is great psychological and therapeutic value in recognizing themes. And I'll speak personally here. I believe that our temperaments, even our rough edges, are part of our funds of knowledge. While I respect the social conventions for how to behave in situations, I often had trouble (or resisted) following through—I'd say the wrong thing, or not know what to say, or not react the way I felt I should. (After all, I wrote a whole book on embarrassment.) There is something contrarian in my core. I'm terrible at following directions—even filling out forms.

For example, at my son's interminable graduation at Boston College, I *knew* the convention was to see this as a significant milestone, a time to celebrate his achievement and appreciate the pomp and circumstance of the ceremony. I could feel that oppressive pride all around me . . . you know, bouquets and rainbow-colored foil balloons. But I was feeling none of that. This had to have been the most boring day of my life, with the endless diplomas to "Sullivan, Sullivan, Sullivan." (It was Boston College.) Real, almost physical pain. When we finally loaded our two cars amid the chaos of the dilapidated mods where my son spent his senior year, I felt like I was escaping a war zone—I was never so happy to get on Interstate 128, aka New England's longest parking lot.

Writing has become, for me, a way to use the rough unconventional edges of my personality. It's one place where they help. In fact, I rely on my quirky autobiography and find that the more I can work it into my writing, the better the reaction. While conventionality is crucial for much of our day-to-day living, it hardly makes for memorable writing. Who wants to read about parents being proud on graduation day? I am not sure that Luis Moll had identity themes—or our personal temperaments—in mind when he developed his concept. It's a stretch for sure.

But it is what we always bring, our unruly selves.

PERMEABLE CURRICULUM

The term *permeable curriulum* is closely related to Moll's great concept. The term comes from child literacy researcher Anne Haas Dyson (2003), and it is illustrated in her classic case study of primary-age African American children, who called themselves "the brothers and the sisters." They saw Dyson as a "fake mama." She describes the "unofficial" worlds of these children, particularly their attraction to TV shows, songs, performers, and especially professional sports teams. (Dyson, not a sports fan herself, had a tutorial with an Oakland Raiders assistant coach to get some background.) The "official world" was the version of writing workshop in their school, with the by-now-familiar features of conferences and sharing among peers. Permeability, then, is the openness of the official curriculum that allows some of the unofficial in, so that we can use it in the school-based expectation for writing. There are, however, tensions about what can come in and when it is appropriate (e.g., football names might not fit a science unit). In her words, a permeable curriculum is "negotiated" and cannot be simply a matter of standards and school-based expectations:

> A permeable curriculum—a negotiated classroom culture—cannot emerge from a *unidirectional* curricular vision. Teachers as well as children must be open, curious, and willing to imagine worlds beyond their own. (1993, 9)

Unlike Moll and his associates, who focused on the skills used in household management, the fund of knowledge that the brothers and sisters bring in comes largely from shared media loyalties.

Dyson also coins another term, *social work*, to describe the ways in which writing about these shared loyalties becomes joint play. Friendship, as she illustrates it, is a profound motivating force for writing. Consequently, writing time is rarely silent—there is often a running commentary, sometimes songs, plans for inviting sports figures to upcoming parties, references to TV shows, rehashing of recent football games, checking the location of football teams on the map, descriptions of what they are writing and drawing.

This use of popular media, however, can meet resistance from those who see such writing as too imitative and inauthentic, especially when compared with genres like memoir.

To these objections, Dyson has powerful rejoinders:

- Children *appropriate* features of popular media; they rarely just copy it. Their texts are often hybrids, where, for example, Buzz Lightyear or Coach Bombay joins the brothers and sisters in some narrative—a process she calls "recontextualization" (2001, 335).
- We can undermine children's early attempts at writing if we view their media affiliations as "dubious in value" (2001, 355)

> or inauthentic. Who is to say that their loyalty to the Dallas Cowboys (America's team during that period) is less authentic (or less useful) than loyalty to a picture book author? Yet, in her view, even progressive approaches like writing workshop fail to value these unofficial resources and the way children use them.
>
> For example, Moll and his coresearchers note, with some irony, that we often view trips to Europe as important educational opportunities but disregard the *regular* international travel of students to Mexico.

Dyson's concept of permeability has broad relevance. Just a survey of the children's shirts attests to media loyalties that often seem inappropriate for schoolwork—too commercial, too popular, too . . . Disney.

But several years ago, I did research in an elementary school that brilliantly mobilized children's media affiliations, specifically their love of Star Wars©. One teacher, herself a Star Wars fan, kept a list of main characters that students could consult as they wrote. The result was exactly the type of hybrid text that Dyson identified, in which kids interwove their friends and Star Wars characters (and their weapons) in their own adventures, page after page. In effect, Star Wars invited the boys in particular into the world of writing, making it social and playful.

MEANINGFUL WRITING PROJECTS

If we shift to the other end of the educational spectrum—college writing—it is easy to imagine the reservation teachers might have about the relevance of funds of knowledge. The writing students do in college is, of course, diverse, but surveys have suggested that there is clearly a shift to a much more objective, impersonal style, with few opportunities for any personal or autobiographical imprint. Professors typically assign tasks that "require recapitulating content for the teacher-examiner reader" (Eodice, Geller, and Lerner 2019, 322; see also Melzer 2014). Academic writing assignments typically promote "the dominance of reason over emotion or sensual perception" (Thaiss and Zawacki 2006, 16).

Indeed, the Common Core State Standards are quite direct in acknowledging that of the three classical components of argument—logos, pathos, and ethos—their focus is logos or reasoning, thus minimizing possibilities for self-presentation (NGA Center for Best Practices and CCSSO 2010). This despite the fact that classical rhetoricians typically gave great weight to ethos—the *self* as presented in an argument. David Coleman (2012), chief architect of the CCSS in ELA, famously put the issue more bluntly in his dismissal of personal forms of writing (specifically memoir and reader response):

> The only problem, forgive me for saying this so bluntly, the only problem with those two forms of writing is as you grow up in this world you realize people really don't give a shit about what you feel or what you think.

Under his direction, the College Board has stressed rhetorical analysis, where the student does not respond to a text but enumerates the rhetorical features, excluding personal opinion about the argument itself.

Teachers who perceive that college writing will entail a shift to largely impersonal writing have grounds for that conclusion and a reason to prepare students for this depersonalized writing. However, there is a growing chorus of writing specialists who have challenged this narrow view of writing, along the same lines that Dyson challenged the impermeable curriculum of elementary schools. I'll focus on two significant studies that tried to determine what made some college-level writing assignments meaningful.

In their award-winning set of case studies, *Persons in Process*, Anne Herrington and Marcia Curtis (2000) closely followed nine students for a full academic year, finally focusing on four of them, whom they followed for their four years of undergraduate writing. Herrington and Curtis describe the struggles of these students, trying to navigate the demands of college writing in such a way that they were *present* in the writing, not passive reporters of information. They struggled, sometimes successfully, sometimes not, to find a way to own the assignments and connect them to their life experience.

In some cases, this meant explicitly referencing these personal experiences. Others, like Rachael, a psychology student, often "veiled" her own experiences as the child of an alcoholic. Yet this personal background shaped the topics she chose to write about—it was an identity theme throughout her undergraduate years. As she worked on the types of writing required in her major, she helped create a professional identity, an authority, and an imagined future where she could make a contribution to dealing with what she called the "disease" of alcoholism. With the encouragement of her professors, she gained the confidence to see her own experiences as valid forms of knowing that she could position with (and against) various theories:

> Sometimes the way we experience things in the world isn't exactly how theories explain things or something you learn in class explains things. I think we experience life differently, writing it down and saying, "Look, this is what the majority of people say, but this is what I found and this is what people I have spoken to have found." Even though that's not written down anywhere, you can certainly make some valid points about what's happened. (in Herrington and Curtis 2000, 268)

Academic writing, as experienced by Rachael, was *permeable*. It was open enough for her to bring in life experiences, to make it meaningful. Herrington and Curtis conclude with an assertion that could serve as a definition of funds of knowledge:

> The combination of recognizing the validity of students' personal knowledge and showing how to bring such knowledge into their academic worlds helps students bridge what may seem like a gaping chasm between themselves and readers, that is, between private and academic pursuits. (377)

While *Persons in Process* explored the personal-public dichotomy through intensive case studies, the Meaningful Writing Project conducted an extensive survey in which 707 students at three universities described undergraduate writing projects they found meaningful (Eodice, Geller, and Lerner 2019). The researchers then coded the responses to determine if there were any common features in the descriptions—and the one that stood out was personal connection.

Personal connection does not necessarily mean writing personal narratives, though it might include that. It refers to "connections to what and who is important in their lives, to their interests, and to their aspirations" (326). For example, writing a collaborative business plan might not seem a kind of personal writing, but students are taking on a role, an identity related to the self they want to be. One student wrote:

> Writing about what was the meaning behind the company and the company's actions and output was inspiring to me. The assignment reconfirmed the reason why I want to be in business. I want to make a difference with what business practices I follow and how I provide a certain good or service to customers. (333–34)

The researchers also found that meaningful writing assignments tended to be "expansive" and "not bounded"; that is, they were open enough, had enough choice for writers to connect with prior interests and experiences. They weren't onetime events on assigned topics unlikely to be revisited in the future. They tapped into more deeply rooted interests and ambitions. For example, in a technical writing class a former army engineer, familiar with various armor systems, investigated the effectiveness of modern safety measures for troops, a continuing concern for him.

The conclusions of the Meaningful Writing Project team are virtually identical to those of Herrington and Curtis:

> We believe the power of personal connections as described by students in our study—namely, the personal connections they make to self, others, and subjects of writing—is a key factor for developing and sustaining student agency and identity in higher learning. (336)

Failure to invite these connections—in the misplaced concern for objectivity and academic rigor—can only create alienation and a dislike of writing, depriving students of a key educational experience. When we don't value this personal connection, we are also devaluing the experience and knowledge of entire communities (Herrington and Curtis 2000, 336).

Which was Moll's point exactly.

TRANSFORMING INFORMATION: THE PLACE OF THE INTERVIEW

I am convinced that we set ourselves up for problems when we ask students to use print resources alone to create a print assignment. The classic report. There may have been a time when locating these print sources was a challenge (e.g., using the card catalogue and that cumbersome *Readers' Guide to Periodical Literature*). But now information is, if anything, too easy to get. When there is no transforming material, what we get is often a pastiche, a reassembling of sources. We can preach about the necessity of putting information into your own words, but the result is often turning secondhand information into thirdhand information. There is no discovery, no creation of information, just a scramble to avoid plagiarism. One way around this problem is to foreground interviewing and use the print sources more for background—what journalists typically do. This poses a challenge for students to transmediate (oral to written), by conducting the interview and then selecting and arranging quotes. (Recall this is what students did when they created the family recipe book.)

Failure to invite these connections—in the misplaced concern for objectivity and academic rigor—can only create alienation and a dislike of writing, depriving students of a key educational experience. (Herrington and Curtis 2000, 336)

I stumbled in this direction when I taught the research essay, a required assignment in first-year writing, typically my least favorite (and least successful) assignment. So, when I taught Malcolm Gladwell's *Outliers*, I asked students to locate someone they knew whom they considered an outlier, someone they felt was an extraordinary achiever, however they wanted to define that. We talked about the questions that might come from Gladwell's book (e.g., the role of luck, the ten thousand hours, mentors). In retrospect, I should have done more prep work like model interviews in class. But what interesting reading.

And such a range of people that my students managed to find, including National Hockey League player Bobby Butler, Red Sox announcer Dave O'Brien, and the woman who brought Curves®, the women's fitness franchise, to Brazil.

The word *text*, like *textile* and *texture*, comes from the Latin root *textere*, "to weave." Writing is rarely purely personal or purely technical and objective—it's a mix, a hybrid, a text. Even when the writer doesn't use *I*, there is the personal fingerprint. In good writing this is often a sense of cognitive energy, manifested in the verbs. We come to writing with a history, what Alfred Tatum calls a "legacy" (2009), and our success (and pleasure) in writing comes from being able to use that history, from believing that we can make writing tasks, even technical ones, our own.

There are benefits for the reader as well. None of us does well with objectivity—it is not a human trait. We need a point of view, we need interwoven stories to see the human reality of any argument, we need some human contact. We need writers to believe that their lived experience counts as evidence, maybe the strongest evidence—that can connect to other kinds of evidence.

Woven.

Chapter Three

TRANSACTIONAL MODEL OF READING

Transactional Model of Reading: The reading of any text—but most especially a literary text—is a transaction in which the reader's intentions, interests, personal background, and pattern of attention play a central role. Reading is an event, an experience, shaped by the text but always unique because each reader approaches the text from a different standpoint. A number of common teaching practices undermine this transaction, particularly ones that predetermine the meaning of the text or reduce the text to information (again often predetermined) to be extracted and tested. To the extent schools focus on analysis, the analysis should build on this experience of reading.

A number of years ago I was teaching an essay on reading to a graduate class of mostly doctoral students, and the author of the essay stressed how a reader should be "aggressive." This term sparked a debate in class that has stayed with me to this day. A woman in the class (who went on to become a major feminist scholar) objected to this term, claiming that it suggested belligerence, even a kind of violence that she connected with distinctive male assertiveness. She, herself, had been subjected to this aggressiveness, and she objected to the term being held up as some kind of ideal. Why should anyone describe reading, an activity she saw as bringing an author and reader together, as having "a fair amount of push and shove" (Bartholomae and Petrosky 2011, 1)?

For full disclosure, I was the editor of the volume in which the essay appeared—and it never occurred to me that anyone would react this way. I saw the term as meaning we should not passively accept what a text says; we should feel entitled to question and challenge ideas we disagree with, just as this student was doing. It felt obvious, benign, constructive—what any good critical reader does. And I regret to say, I didn't even bother to imagine that I was reading as a man, one who as a child did a fair amount of pushing and shoving on the playground (I was rarely the one pushed). I appreciate now that this was a masculinist perspective, even a macho one, that could be offensive.

The word evoked such different reactions, different histories, a basic feature of our language use. Louise Rosenblatt writes:

> Part of the magic—and indeed of the essence—of language is the fact that it must be internalized by each individual human being, with all the special overtones that each unique person and unique situation entail. (1978, 20)

Since this is the very "essence" of language, texts—even academic ones like the one I was using in my class—cannot have a determinate meaning. Even the writer of the essay could not control the associations the student made; he could not anticipate how the term *aggressive* would call up her history or how it would be so dramatically different from mine and from his.

Rosenblatt, whose transactional model[1] is the subject of this chapter, had bad timing in her scholarly career. Her first book, *Literature as Exploration*, which examines the complex dynamics of reader response, came out in 1938, just as New Criticism became the dominant mode of analysis in schools and colleges. With New Criticism, the focus was on the "text itself," on form, imagery, and analysis that often seemed to have

1. The term *transactional* is now often used to describe a relationship that is self-interested and coldly pragmatic. Such a meaning is diametrically different from the one Rosenblatt proposes.

no relationship to the moment-by-moment experience of reading. In fact, some New Critics claimed it was a fallacy to conflate the literary work with the effect it had on the individual reader; the text was an autonomous object, stable and open, and not to be reduced to the "impressionism" of the individual reader (Wimsatt and Beardsley 1949).

In the hands of skilled teachers, this new practice of close readings could be exhilarating and could provide ways of appreciating the complex poetry being written at the time. Not all proponents dismissed the emotional reactions of the reader. I. A. Richards, author of the hugely influential *Practical Criticism*, claimed there was a place for the emotional reaction of the reader:

> The personal situation of the reader inevitably (and within limits rightly) affects his reading. . . . Though it has been fashionable—in deference to sundry confused doctrines of "pure art" and "impersonal aesthetic emotions"—to deplore such a state of affairs, there is really no occasion. For a comparison of the feelings active in a poem with some personal feeling still present in the reader's lively recollection does give a standard, a test for reality. (1929, 239)

Richards cautions, though, that the role of the poem is to "*control and order* such feelings" (239) and not simply to "arouse" them.

But in reality, the student readers were at a considerable disadvantage in this game, putting their naïve and hesitant interpretations up against those of an instructor who had expert knowledge. Often, students had to create these readings with little biographical knowledge about the writer (that would be another fallacy), and sometimes they read the poem without knowing the author—a common technique popularized by Richards. The result was a power imbalance that literary scholar Robert Scholes satirizes:

> In the name of improved interpretation, reading was turned into a mystery and the literature classroom into a chapel where the priestly instructor (who knows the authors, dates, titles, biographies, and general provenance of the

> texts) astounded the faithful with miracles of interpretation. (1982, 15)

I sat in classes where these performances took place—and I couldn't begin to imagine the *process* that produced these readings. It reminded me of an old Maine joke: the lost traveler asks at a country store how to get to Castine, and the storekeeper answers, "You can't get there from here." That's how I felt.

In my own classes of prospective English teachers, I regularly asked if any of their literature teachers ever demonstrated how they read a text *for the first time*. Invariably the answer was no. And I thought, *How strange*. This, after all, is what they were asking students to do, to wrestle with often difficult texts that they had never read before, and the teachers never—not once—modeled this fundamental transaction for the students. Rosenblatt's career was a long battle to argue for reading as a transaction—and to reject New Critical views of the objective, autonomous text, seemingly impervious to the role of the reader.

THE TEXT ITSELF

Of course, questions about the authority and definitiveness of texts have been around as long as there have been texts. Plato expressed anxiety that writing, unaccompanied by the author, would be misread, "ill-treated and unjustly abused" (2005, 63). He compared it to sending unprotected children out into the world. For centuries, the Bible was available only to those who read Latin—and the meaning of this sacred book was controlled by church dogma. This control was threatened by the emergence of the printing press in the late fifteenth century and even more so by the actual printing of the Bible in the vernacular, most notably Martin Luther's German translation. This innovation allowed direct access to scripture, unmediated by ritual, priests, or Catholic dogma. The French essayist Michel de Montaigne warned that the "novelties of Luther" would lead common readers astray by "chance appearance," thus undermining the "awesomeness of ancient custom" (1987, 490). By the time Montaigne was writing, he claimed this unmediated reading had already created schisms—"discords and doubts" (1213)—and even warfare among competing sects.

This same anxiety about certainty and the limits of interpretation pervade the Common Core State Standards. In a guide to publishers, the main authors of the CCSS English language arts section invoke the language of the most severe New Critics. Student readers are to stay, at least initially, within "the four corners of the text" (Coleman and Pimentel 2012, 4): they are to understand the text "on its own terms" (9) and not employ any outside information or frames of reference. Indeed, they recommend 80 to 90 percent of the questions on the reading be "text-dependent" (6)—that is, answerable without drawing on outside sources such as prior reading or life experience. (This rule, in practice, will surely lead to a lot of right-or-wrong questions!) In order to stay within these strictures, a common writing form for examinations is the rhetorical analysis, where students explicate the techniques used by the writer but do not make any judgment about the argument itself (which would involve too much subjectivity). They stay within the four corners of the text.

In an *Education Week* commentary, my colleague Maja Wilson and I (2011) objected to this conception of reading. Language, we argued, by its very nature invokes our experiences—as the term *aggressive* did in my class. It is simply impossible to disengage our history, our values, and our biases and attend the text itself, and I can't imagine a writer who would want that from a reader. The great Roman essayist Seneca recognized this fact.

The authors of the CCSS guide regularly use the term *extract* to describe the process of reading and view the text as a *repository*. Clearly there are texts we may treat this way, but the complex texts the CCSS want in school require a much more sustained interactive process in which the readers make their mark—often literally. David Bartholomae and Anthony Petrosky are clear on what we expect in college reading:

> A danger arises in assuming that reading is only a search for information or main ideas. . . . Student readers, for example, can take responsibility for determining the meaning of the text. They can work as though they were doing something

There is nothing particularly surprising about this way which everyone has of deriving material for their own individual interests from identical subject matter. In one and the same meadow the cow looks for grass, the dog for the hare, and the stork for the lizard.

— Seneca

> other than finding ideas already there on the page, and they can be guided by their own impressions and questions as they read. (2011, 6)

Reading, they assert, "is not simply a matter of hanging back and waiting for a piece, or its author, to tell you what the writing has to say" (1).

In our own response, Maja Wilson and I pointed out what we saw as the central flaw in the four-corners model. We agreed with the goals of close reading and students developing interesting claims—with evidence—about texts. But perversely, the standards close off access to the kinds of prior knowledge and questions (all outside the four corners) that would enable students to form interesting claims:

> While the virtues of a close reading are many, there is no guidance given in this document for how students will create the questions, hypotheses, or interpretations necessary to generate an interesting claim about a text. In fact, many of the activities useful for generating these claims are expressly limited. (2011)

As an example, imagine that a student reading *The Great Gatsby* objected to the way Gatsby treats Daisy and said that he is, in his own way, just as domineering and controlling as her abusive husband, Tom. I think any American lit teacher would find this a provocative claim, with the student working against the more conventional perception that Gatsby is, well, great. But to create this claim, the student would have to draw on social intelligence, on empathy, on norms of behavior, which *are not in the text*. The reader would need to imagine how humiliating it might be for Daisy, in the sweltering hotel room, to be pressured by Gatsby to say she never loved her husband, Tom.

We concluded that helping students *understand* the text itself means helping students find themselves in it—not to suppress the self, but to engage the self: "All the instruction in the world won't help a reader who has already decided that a text is distant and irrelevant." In fact, if we look at the derivation of *understand*, it means to "be among" or "in the midst of"—which is where Rosenblatt wants to place readers.

THE READER, THE TEXT, AND THE POEM

When we think of poems, we naturally think of a kind of text with stanzas, line breaks, a form that we can analyze. It has an objective existence. To understand Rosenblatt's transactional model, it is necessary to abandon this conception. She distinguishes the text (the objective marks on the page) from the poem, which is the *experience* of readers as they bring their histories, biases, and patterns of attention into play and they transact with the text.

> The poem, then, must be thought of as an event in time. It is not an object or an ideal entity. It happens during a coming-together, a compenetration, of a reader and a text. The reader brings to the text his past experience and present personality. Under the magnetism of the ordered symbols of the text, he marshals his resources and crystallizes out from the stuff of memory, thought, and feeling, a new order, a new experience, which he sees as the poem. (1978, 12)

Every reading—every poem—then, is a unique experience, as readers approach the same text from different standpoints: age, gender, ethnicity, life experience, and so much more. We have all had the experience of rereading a book after a span of years and having a completely different reaction. This happened to me with my rereading of Hemingway's *A Farewell to Arms*, which I found so romantic when I read it in college and so disappointing, the love story in particular, when I read it later.

One of the most attractive features of her transactional model is the way she frees reading from what Scholes called the priesthood of academic interpretation. She upends the presumption that there are codes and theories, unavailable to the common reader, that are essential to understanding. To be fair, I have had instructors who honored our naïve readings—one in particular, a classics teacher who said to us: "I really envy you because you are going to have an experience I can no longer have. You will be reading *The Iliad* for the first time."

The most critical funds of knowledge we possess as readers (and humans!) is our ability to read behavior, to judge and name it. The words we use are probably the most important vocabulary we possess. These words function as interpretive lenses. Is he being obnoxious or just outgoing, maybe a free spirit? What is the dividing line, the distinction between reckless and daring? Sad and depressed? Aggressive and assertive? So much of our social life involves making these behavioral judgments. In fact, that is what gossip generally is: a story and a judgment. The inability to reliably judge social behavior is a tremendous liability often associated with the autism spectrum.

If the poem—the moment-by-moment experience of reading—is not a thing but an event, that poses issues for how we teach (and how we assess reading). As you might imagine, Rosenblatt has no patience for standardized reading tests. Can there be any more systematic sabotage of the reading experience than this?

- To present the reader with a text (no choice, no context, often an excerpt, sometimes modified),
- to predetermine the correct or ideal outcome of the reading, and
- to put the reader under time pressure to achieve that reading.

When the goal is to answer questions at the end of a reading, test takers often look at the questions first and then look for the answers in the text—which is hardly reading at all.

When we are fully engaged with reading, when we are in the zone, we almost lose touch with our surroundings and with time itself. We are into the book—as one of Jeff Wilhelm's (1996) students put it, "You gotta *be* the book." We feel we know the characters, even that we are accompanying them; we wince at their bad decisions; we feel a comfort with the narrator and feel ourselves in rhythm with the way the story is unfolding. Another student, actually a struggling reader, put it this way:

> When I'm in the reading zone, I feel like I'm a character in the book I'm reading. When I'm in my reading zone it's almost like a TV show or a movie. I can see it really well. I can feel, taste, see, smell when I'm in my reading zone.

> Everything around you disappears and all you care about are the characters. (Atwell and Merkel 2009, 24)

When we are in this zone, any interruption is irritating, and when we finish reading there is often a momentary sense of disorientation, as if we are not quite ready to leave.

So what are teachers to do? If the ideal state of reading is so immersive, an optimal experience of flow, isn't any teaching strategy a form of disruption? Isn't any request for reflection or analysis a distraction? How can we teach and still respect—even enhance—the reading experience?

WHAT READERS DO

Rosenblatt's model upends common assumptions about the way we should teach literature. It is common to assume that only certain texts are complex enough, serious enough, to create a meaningful experience for the reader. Even if the reader struggles and dislikes the text, time spent with the book is considered worthwhile; it creates familiarity and cultural capital. By contrast, the more popular, contemporary, more easily accessible books that students might prefer are seen as escapist, predictable, and just too damn easy to read. But for Rosenblatt, the true test is the journey a book takes the reader on.

Jeffrey Wilhelm and Michael Smith also challenge these elitist assumptions in their groundbreaking book *Reading Unbound* (2014). They show how genres generally considered subliterature, for example, vampire novels, can elicit deeply engaged, thoughtful readings. They ask these provocative questions:

> Might kids gravitate to the kinds of texts they need? Might they experience a deep fulfillment that we don't completely understand when they read those books? Might passionate readers of marginalized texts—those books that many parents and teachers disapprove of at some level—be choosing books that help them build on new interests, become competent in new ways, and grow beyond their current selves? (9)

The obverse is also true: texts should not hold their place in the curriculum irrespective of experiences students have reading them.

Or often not reading them.

I know of no reliable study of the reading avoidance of class-assigned novels, but it is surely considerable. In a set of interviews with her own high school students, Penny Kittle found them very open about their strategies, often a combination of using class discussion and Sparknotes®, maybe combined with some reading of the book to "get quotes" (Kittle 2010). And often this was enough to be successful on tests and even in writing papers.

The alternative, first elaborated by Nancie Atwell in her classic *In the Middle* (2015), is to begin not by identifying books that students should read, but by looking at the conditions that support committed reading—and creating a culture of reading in the classroom. The most obvious condition is *choice*. Choice of authors and genres, to be sure. But also choosing the right pace of reading—time of day, length of reading periods; we even have preferences for how we like to sit, the lighting, the very feel of the book. My son will not read hardbacks—too heavy and awkward. (Doris Kearns Goodwin tells the story of a man who fell asleep while reading her weighty biography of Lincoln: the book slipped, breaking his nose.) Typically, we share reading recommendations and enjoy conversations about books read in common, either informally or in book groups. That's what readers do. So how can a classroom build some of these choices into a reading curriculum? I devote a full chapter (Chapter 8, "Independent Reading") to that question.

THE ART OF PAYING ATTENTION

Let's start with the obvious: in any text there are more possible points of attention than a reader could attend to—or that an author could control. Our brains are wired to do a lot of forgetting, but we do hold on to gists and moments that strike us as significant. And one of the pleasures of sharing our experiences of reading is that different readers will notice different things, and the text becomes fuller, richer.

Years ago I was watching an Orson Welles production of *Macbeth*, and my six-year-old son managed to watch some of it with me. Later that afternoon, we were visiting a friend of mine and she asked Andy what he thought of *Macbeth*. "It's about these little kids who get killed." *Little kids who get killed?* At first I was puzzled, and then I remembered the very short scene, seconds actually, where McDuff's wife and children are killed. That *would* register with a six-year-old, and upon reflection it shows the level of cruelty Macbeth was capable of.

On another occasion, I was working with a group of teachers on what I called "slow reading." I read the beginning of books slowly, trying to get the feel of the narrator and the language and beginning to form judgments about characters. In this case we were reading the wonderful opening of Jennifer Egan's novel *A Visit from the Goon Squad* (2010), where we meet Sasha, a kleptomaniac trying to explain to her psychiatrist why she stole a woman's wallet in a hotel bathroom:

> It began the usual way, in the bathroom of the Lassimo Hotel. Sasha was adjusting her yellow eye shadow in the mirror when she noticed a bag on the floor beside the sink that must have belonged to the woman whose peeing she could faintly hear through the vaultlike door of the toilet stall. Inside the rim of the bag, barely visible, was a wallet made of pale green leather. It was easy for Sasha to recognize. Looking back, the peeing woman's blind trust provoked her. (3)

We all shared what struck us in the opening. My attention was drawn to the way Sasha rationalized her theft: it was really the "peeing woman's "trust" that provoked her.

But one woman in our group mentioned the yellow eye shadow: "Yellow eye shadow. Yellow eye shadow. It doesn't make you look very good. Who wears yellow eye shadow?"

Another followed up: "Yeah, and yellow eye shadow in the bathroom of a hotel, and it sounds like she is in there a lot. You know, I think she's a prostitute." Which, it turned out, was not a bad prediction. Yet for me that detail did not register at all—I lacked any cosmetic frame of reference to pick it up.

Revisiting a text to look more closely at a scene is a type of reexperiencing that can enhance the aesthetic pleasure of reading. We move through a text so quickly that we may pass over a detail like the yellow eye shadow. By going back to these moments in the text, we can note new details that we missed the first time around. I also think it is a very congenial way of responding, something we naturally do anyway. In my college days, W. C. Fields was all the rage and my friends and I would perform great lines, imitating his voice, in the Oberlin evening: "I cook with wine. Sometimes I even add it to the food."

I asked Robert Probst, one of the earliest and savviest promoters of Rosenblatt's transactional model (1988), how he started discussion, and it was reassuringly similar to what I had stumbled on:

> *I ask the students what they observed in the text that caused them to pause, to raise questions. What was it that stopped you? What did you notice that you think merits discussion? I asked students to pay attention to themselves as they read so they could come prepared to share something they had observed in the text.*

Generations of readers, for example, have been convinced that they lack the background or critical skills to read modern poetry. There is some code we lack, some set of terms we failed to learn (what is a sestina, after all?). But if we adopt Probst's starting point, we have an inviting way in.

In my work with teachers, I often gave them Jane Kenyon's poem "Let Evening Come" (1990). I asked them to read it through two or three times and in the latter readings to note a word that struck them—maybe a particularly vivid word, or one that powerfully recalled their own experience, or one that clarified the poem for them. I emphasized that there could be many points of attention. I told them that we would share the words we chose and say something about why we chose them. I invite you to do the same:

Let Evening Come

Let the light of late afternoon
shine through chinks in the barn, moving
up the bales as the sun moves down.

Let the cricket take up chafing
as a woman takes up her needles
and her yarn. Let evening come.

Let dew collect on the hoe abandoned
in long grass. Let the stars appear
and the moon disclose her silver horn.

Let the fox go back to its sandy den.
Let the wind die down. Let the shed
go black inside. Let evening come.

To the bottle in the ditch, to the scoop
in the oats, to air in the lung
let evening come.

Let it come, as it will, and don't
be afraid. God does not leave us
comfortless, so let evening come.

Each time I do this, a different word calls my attention. This time it is *evening*, a particularly soothing word, much more so than *night*, which is so much more abrupt and harsh. Evening comes on slowly; it is more an experience, a witnessing of the fading of the light, the lengthening shadows, the sunset. Because the work of the day is done, we can be still and contemplate it.

As we shared words, the poem became fuller. Participants have nominated *chafing*, a kind of discordant sound in such a peaceful poem. Some recalled barns from their childhood, with the light seeping in. And of course, there is *Let*. Evening will come, of course, whether we let it come or not—so how do we read *Let*? Once we were done sharing, we read the poem aloud Quaker style—I read the first stanza and stopped, then, someone read the next stanza and we continued to "let evening come."

I have also found that it is important to stay close to the particularity of the text, the language and details of behavior, and not to leap to theory or theme, to ideas or a moral message. When we jump to theory—for example, when we say that a relationship is oedipal or a plot is an archetype—the work often loses its particularity, its proper density. It becomes an *example* of a something else, and discussion often ends. When we see Jay Gatsby as a symbol or example of the American dream, we reduce him from a character to an idea, which flattens out the discordant pieces of his personality.

This leap to theory or theme has another disadvantage: it seems to privilege a kind of formal sociological knowledge or terminology that the "common reader" does not possess. It just sounds smarter. But I would argue, along with Rosenblatt, that the tacit, experience-based, unofficial, everyday theories that we all can bring to texts are really far richer and more complex. And they keep the text open.

When we jump to theory—for example, when we say that a relationship is oedipal or a plot is an archetype—the work often loses its particularity, its proper density.

RESPONSE, RESPONSIBILITY, EXPERIENCE

As Rosenblatt's theory became popular in the 1980s, it was often associated with *reader response*, a term she never felt entirely comfortable with. There is, of course, its association with behaviorism: stimulus-response. It suggests a sequence—I do something, and you respond—which is not at all an apt description of the reading transaction, which is more of an ongoing, lived-through *experience*. The term *experience* for Dewey (1934), a foundational figure for Rosenblatt, does not mean simple activity or habitual and repeated behavior. Experience has a shape: a pattern of problem leading to solution, tension to resolution. It is purpose driven and not simply random or impressionistic. It is not simply a reaction or a response: it is an *undergoing*, a time-bound narrative experience, heightened under the control of the artist or novelist, but present for the scientist, inventor, craftsperson, sportscaster, and grant writer as well. It requires sustained attention and an openness to what is unfolding.

While Rosenblatt's major contribution was reclaiming a role for the reader, there comes with it an obligation to attend to "signposts" (Beers and Probst 2014, 2016). There are established ways that authors draw our attention to what they feel is significant—titles, repetitions, beginnings, endings, key words, plot shifts, relationships, setting and its effect on the characters, conflicts, change and growth in the characters. My former colleague Gary Lindberg stressed the importance of immediacy in our reading, attending to the small and particular. In one prompt, he asked students to evaluate a decision a character made:

> For each character involved describe what the character *could say* or *could do* but chooses not to. Explain as clearly as you can why the characters behave as they do. (1986, 150)

To be responsible is to pay attention, to be open to novelty, to change. It is to engage our own histories but also to recognize that we are encountering something new—we don't just project ourselves onto the text.

Suppose we try this out with a seemingly minor incident in *The Great Gatsby*: the decision about who drives in which car after the tumultuous confrontation in the New York City hotel room. Daisy's husband, Tom, insists that Daisy goes with Gatsby—even though the whole purpose of the New York excursion, in Gatsby's mind, was to announce that Daisy was leaving Tom. One might have expected Tom to say that she would be returning to Long Island with him. I mean, a man has just threatened to take your wife away and you send her back to Long Island with him? Lindberg invites us to speculate why.

We might also look at the decision to allow Daisy to drive back—Gatsby later explains it was to "steady her" (Fitzgerald 1995, 151). "Steady her"? They had been drinking, she was distraught, and even then traffic could be heavy out of Manhattan. The most obvious and prudent choice would have been for Gatsby to drive—and for Daisy to calm her nerves as a passenger. Why would he decide this (and it did seem his decision)? We can't be sure if Gatsby would have avoided the deadly accident with Myrtle Wilson, Tom's mistress, but clearly Daisy was unfit to drive. And is there a pattern of similarly poor decisions on this day? Why would someone who had had such spectacular success up to this point make so many misjudgments?

In my interview with Bob Probst, he argued that "responsibility" may be a more significant idea for Rosenblatt than "response." She had no patience with what she saw as the relativism that equated all readings, even inattentive ones. To be responsible is to pay attention, to be open to novelty, to change. It is to engage our own histories but also to recognize that we are encountering something new—we don't just project ourselves onto the text. It is being able to flexibly enter into the experience of others, to test out our value system as we encounter new situations—and possibly adjust those values, extend our range of understanding and sympathy. In the process, we create something new, something that did not exist prior to our reading.

My colleague Gary Lindberg, whom I have already cited, focused on this kind of reading at the end of his life. An Americanist, he had already established himself as an important scholar, but as he was finishing his last scholarly work, on the confidence man in American literature, he was diagnosed with leukemia. He and his doctors managed to control it for years, but his illness became active in the mid-1980s.

In the last months of his life he turned his back on the kind of scholarship he had excelled at—and he began to write about the more everyday, naïve act of reading, which, after all, was what he focused on in his classroom. He focused on what Virginia Woolf called "the common reader":

> The common reader, as Dr. Johnson implies, differs from the critic and the scholar. . . . He reads for his own pleasure rather than to impart knowledge or correct the opinions of others. Above all, he is guided by an instinct to create for himself, out of whatever odds and ends he can come by, some kind of whole. (Woolf 1925)

Like Samuel Johnson, she claims that it is the common reader, not the critic or scholar, who ultimately determines the lasting value of books.

Sadly, Gary lost the race with his disease and managed only one essay, which he delivered at a conference I organized. I remember him delivering it, thin, frail, and obviously dying. The talk was included in a collection I edited, though I didn't touch a word he wrote. The ending of his essay encapsulates everything my own chapter is struggling to say. So I'll close with it:

> There is perhaps something to be said for those truths about texts that supposedly hold their shape independent of the biases of particular readers. They satisfy our wish for something stable, authoritative, and pure. But they are also dead. By their very nature they are irrelevant to the human needs of readers. There is much more to be said for those messier truths that we formulate, undo, and remake again and again in the human gesture of coming to words. Such truths never last. They are too tentative to connect in elaborate systems of meaning. But they renew our acquaintance with the things of the world, they loosen our bondage to a fixed perspective, and they open us up to the endless surprise of dialogue with someone else. (Lindberg 1986, 156)

Credo

I believe in the power and pleasure of slow reading. I believe in the importance of sound in reading—of rhythm, emphasis, even silence—and that when we fail to hear these sounds, even internally, we have lost something important. I believe in authors and my relationship to them and that all serious relationships require commitment and attention. I believe this capacity for attentive reading is a central mission of education, one that unites all fields of study—indeed, I believe most learning is about being deliberate, slowing down; otherwise, we are only reinforcing what we already know. I believe that slow reading runs counter to a media culture that stresses speed, distraction, and a loss of history. I believe in works of literature that have endured and that it is a great gift to students to make this work accessible and meaningful. I also believe in the power of great contemporary literature and think it is critical to acknowledge these writers, as the song advises, "in their living years." And I look forward to the time when we return to naming schools, parks, and bridges after authors.

All this I believe.

Lee Speedway

For a couple years, when I first moved to Durham I would hear, on Friday nights, a noise coming from the west. I thought it might be from the race track in Lee, but decided it couldn't be - the track was 6 miles away. This sound was loud and close, a rumble of ebb and flow acceleration, deceleration

But is was the supermodified cars at the Speedway that I was hearing, that kept children in Lee awake on Friday night. Since I have begun going there I have come to love that noise. The supermodified cars look like overgrown go carts with a big air foil on back to steady them on curves. They reach a top speed of 130 m.p.h on a third of a mile track with straightaways less than of only 150 yard. They circle the track in about 8 seconds.

But it is the noise more than the speed that I love. The noise attacks you, shortens your breath, it hurts. You feel it all over your body. not just in your ears. It surrounded and pressed on you drowning everything. You couldn't even shout in the ear of the person next to you and be heard. You have to brace yourself for the attack as the cars go around the curves and when the race is done, there is relief.

Chapter Four

THE WRITING PROCESS

The Writing Process: The texts that we read do not reveal the process that went into their creation. Or, as Don Murray put it more graphically: "Process cannot be inferred from product any more than a *pig* can be inferred from a *sausage*." Unless we reveal that process (and teach it), students might imagine that writers have some magical talent, that words simply pour out in their final form. We can demystify the act of writing by looking to the accounts that practicing writers give—and building opportunities for students to engage in similar practices in a workshop classroom. Although writing can sometimes feel like magic, it is more often the result of engaging in a frequently messy process, working from initial conception, to drafting, to revision, to editing (often with recursive loops backward). Proponents of the writing process stress that the myth of talent can hold us back and that what matters most is engaging in a workmanlike process.

Second grader Allan described his new understanding of writing after having spent most of the year in a classroom where children authored books:

> Before I ever wrote a book I used to think there was a big machine, and they typed the title and then the machine went until the book was done. Now I look at a book and know that a guy wrote it. And it's been his project for a long time. After the guy writes it, he probably thinks about questions people will ask him and revises it like I do and xeroxes it to about six editors. Then he fixes it up like how they say. (Newkirk 1988, 159)

Allan explained several key principles in writing process instruction:

- ***Identity:*** Allan sees himself as doing what other authors do. He *is* an author, a maker of books, and not simply a student, doing schoolwork, getting ready—someday—to write. He knows that writing demands sustained effort. At the time he made this comment (around 1981), it was generally assumed that primary-age children were not ready to write; they might dictate stories or write about a common classroom experience using words from a class chart. This "language experience approach" was then the cutting edge of children's writing (Van Allen and Allen 1982). But many thought they were not ready for the full, unscaffolded act of writing.
- ***Audience:*** Allan is writing for an audience; he is concerned with "questions people will ask." He knows his books will be part of a classroom library and circulate among his classmates.
- ***Process:*** He knows that writing is a human process, not the magical act of onetime creation. It has been demystified for him. He (and other authors) go through stages of creation and revision in order to meet readers' expectations.
- ***Opportunity:*** For Allan and his classmates, writing was a regular activity. Donald Graves (1983), who oversaw the shift in writing instruction at Allan's school, stressed that regular and sustained practice was essential—he could

> be scathing (and really funny) about what he called the "cha, cha, cha" curriculum, so crowded that students were always *transitioning*. He would sometimes do a dance to illustrate.

It is hardly a surprising claim that writing is a process. After all, every activity is a process—brushing your teeth, loading an update on your computer. The bare claim of writing as a process hardly hints at the tectonic shift in writing instruction being advocated—and why this was a profoundly democratic shift. Nor does it hint at the obstacles in the way.

TALENT AND TIME

When I was collecting stories about the emergence of the writing process movement at UNH, my friend Maureen Barbieri recounted an early experience with Don Murray:

> *He was so reassuring. When I was an undergrad, he told me I had "talent." When I puffed out my chest, grinning, he said, "It doesn't mean much. People like me get published because people like you sit on your hands."*

It sounds a little harsher than I suspect it was. And Maureen did later go on to publish an award-winning book on girls' writing.

But it was a point Don made in many ways. That we have to dispel the idea that the world can be divided between the untalented (a huge majority) and the talented (a gifted few). And for those with the gift, writing comes easily, almost spontaneously. Moreover, those with talent do not suffer the doubts (e.g., the imposter complex) that the rest of us have to deal with. They never reach that point when they are disgusted, literally nauseated, with their writing. In Allan's terms, their minds work "like a big machine and they typed the title, and then the machine went until the book was done."

For his entire life Murray collected writers' testimonies that dismantled this myth. Those who appear talented know how to engage in a process. Writing is not about having (or not having) talent—what Carol

Dweck (2007) later called a fixed mindset. It is about knowing how to engage in a process in which you break a complex task into manageable parts, and it is about the willingness to work through that process. Or as Stephen King put it: "Talent is cheaper than table salt. What separates the talented individual from the successful one is a lot of hard work" (in Beckett 1996, 19). It follows, I believe, that this view opens up possibilities for anyone willing to commit to a process. Writing is democratically possible. For Nancie Atwell the writing process affirms "that anyone, given enough time and practical help, can write well, can be a writer." It is no accident that Peter Elbow, one of the leaders of this movement, titled his collected essays *Everyone Can Write*.

We need to fight for basic simplicity of the rhetorical triangle—someone writing something to someone.

But in order for students to have these opportunities, teachers need to carve out space in the school day for extensive writing practice. An impetus for change was the alarmist 1975 *Newsweek* cover story "Why Johnny Can't Write" (Sheils). Johnny's perennial troubles with reading had apparently spread to his writing. The article prompted the Ford Foundation to fund Donald Graves' review of writing instruction in schools. He titled his report "Balance the Basics: Let Them Write" (1978/2013) and argued that an impediment to teaching writing was the almost complete dominance of reading in the language arts curriculum and in teacher preparation. In Peter Elbow's memorable phrase, writing had to fight for its half of the bed. And even when writing occurred, it was often a part of a reading program, or used to assess reading, those disagreeable questions at the end of a passage. In high school, writing was often used to analyze or explicate literary texts. In effect, writing—when it existed at all—was colonized by reading.

Then there is the problem of *stuff*. Writing can be easily crowded out of the curriculum by writing-like materials, sometimes called peripherals. The disadvantage of writing from a purely commercial standpoint is that it doesn't need stuff. Just something to write on and something to write with. Where is the market here? But peripherals—spelling programs, vocabulary programs, grammar units, formative tests, digital platforms for recording progress—are tangible and sellable and can feed the educational-industrial complex. Moreover, they can also feed digital platforms like PowerSchool®, which invite regular grades and scores that hovering parents can monitor in real time. We need to fight for basic simplicity of the rhetorical triangle—someone writing something to someone.

Graves marshalled a number of arguments for this balancing:

- ***Civic:*** It is a skill needed for democratic participation.
- ***Cognitive:*** It enhances thinking.
- ***Personal Courage:*** "Writers leave the shelter of anonymity and offer to public scrutiny their interior language, feelings and thoughts" (1978, 22). While reading can remain a private act, writing almost invariably is public, even if we are only silently reading our own writing, exposing our writing self to our reading self.

In my interview with Nancie Atwell, she listed these "orthodoxies Donald Graves upended":

- *Young children can't write.*
- *Writing is an exercise orchestrated by a teacher.*
- *Children don't have ideas and experiences to write about; they don't have intentions.*
- *Writing is first-time final.*
- *Writing is homework.*
- *Children need to learn parts of speech, sentence types, handwriting, proper spelling, and paragraphing* before *they can write.*
- *Reading comes before writing.*
- *Writing is a solitary process, and conferring and getting assistance are cheating.*
- *Students write for the teacher and for a grade.*
- *There is one genre—the "school essay."*
- *Students don't care about writing, and they naturally don't like it.*

> *The ability to write is a gift, possessed by the talented few, rather than a teachable craft.*

Interestingly, one of his most compelling arguments was that writing can enhance reading competence. While reading doesn't necessarily involve writing, writing involves reading—in fact, it is virtually impossible to write without reading your own text. One of Donald Murray's great disappointments was the failure of reading researchers to explore the reading that goes on in the writing process.

The most dramatic contribution, in my view, is aiding children to break the symbol-sound code. There is unanimity among reading researchers about the significance of phonemic awareness—the ability to recognize that words are made up of a sequence of significant sounds that can match up to written letters.

Traditionally it was thought that writing played little role in this process; children did very little writing in the primary grades, and in none of that writing did they really explore the writing system. Traditionally, teachers expected children from the very beginning to write every word correctly, with all the directionality and spacing conventionally correct. In other words, they allowed for none of the approximation that characterizes the way we learn to talk.

This restriction dramatically limited what they might say—and it foreclosed attempts they might make to work out phonemic relationships. Take, for example, the written debate I had with my six-year-old daughter (see Figure 4.1). It occurred when I kept her from going into the bedroom she shared with her sister to get her leotard. Her sister was taking a nap and I thought I could put off the intrusion. In the second page (!) of the argument, my daughter proceeded to demolish me.

If, for example, we look at the word *leotard* at the bottom of the page (not a typical first-grade vocabulary word), we will notice that it is misspelled. Not conventional. But this six-year-old is figuring out a lot about sound-symbol connections. She has divided the word into its three syllables; she has accounted for all the phonemes that we hear ("lee a trrd"). The same goes for *another* ("onu Thr") and *about* ("ABOT") and *brain* ("BRAN"). She comes close with *thinking's* ("tikins") and *want*

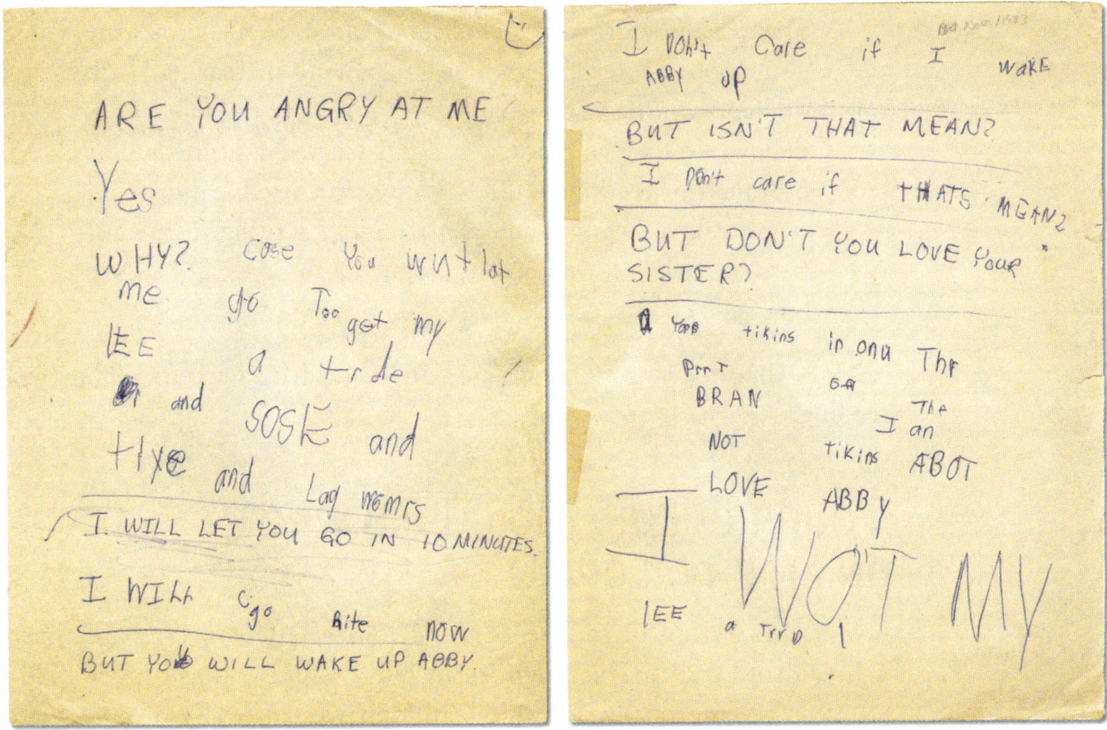

ARE YOU ANGRY AT ME

Yes

WHY? Cose You wunt let me go Too get my LEE a trde and SOSE and tIYe and Lag wemrs

I WILL LET YOU GO IN 10 MINUTES.

I WILL go Rite now

BUT YOU WILL WAKE UP ABBY.

I Don't Care if I wake ABBY up

BUT ISN'T THAT MEAN?

I Don't care if THATS MEAN?

BUT DON'T YOU LOVE YOUR SISTER?

Yore tikins in ona Thr Prn T BRAN OR NOT The I an tikins ABOT LOVE ABBY

I WOT MY LEE a Trrd!

Figure 4.1 ***Child's Debate with Author about Retrieving Socks, Tights, and Leotard from the Room She Shared with Her Sister***

("wot"). She even—quite dramatically—shows emphasis by writing in huge letters as well as using the conventional exclamation point. As she does more reading, a visual image of words will replace this sounded-out version. But what rich possibilities for expression (and argumentation) are opened up.

Graves' argument also anticipates a cultural phenomenon, what Deborah Brandt has called the rise of writing. Writing, she argues, has become the ascendant skill, as demands for documentation increase and platforms for writing proliferate. Where in the past there were editorial gatekeepers for fiction distributions, now there are literally millions of fan-fiction versions of the Harry Potter® books online. Schools, she argues, are out of touch with this cultural shift:

> The rise of writing presents its greatest challenge to the educational enterprise, which is growing increasingly out of step with the wider world. From its start the school has defined literacy as reading and has treated writing skill as a branch of reading skill. Although recent educational initiatives have begun to emphasize more writing in the curriculum, writing remains untaught or undertaught in the nation's schools. (2015, 165)

It is time for writing to assume at least parity with its alpha twin, reading.

A CURRICULUM YOU COULD WRITE ON AN ENVELOPE

It is time for writing to assume at least parity with its alpha twin, reading.

In the Declaration of Independence, Thomas Jefferson boldly claimed "self-evident" truths. This might seem like a slippery evasion. Shouldn't all ideas be empirically derived? Shouldn't we trust only ones that are tested this way? Aren't some ideas self-evident to some but contestable to others? Yet I would argue that there are some teaching principles that are self-evidently beneficial. We sometimes call them nonnegotiable. In reality, as we actually live our lives, we rely on plausibility more than on research evidence. And the test of plausibility is this: Can we frame a believable argument in opposition?

This is a preamble to the core principles of the writing process approach as they were formulated in the early 1980s. These were elegantly economical and self-evident in the way I have described—and they have weathered well over the past nearly half century. The three key principles were time, choice, and response. At the risk of muddying this trinity, I would like to expand it somewhat, trying to retain a sense of economy.

Several years ago, I did a presentation on clutter in our educational system, the piling up of concepts, programs, materials, tests, data—to the point where, if we could create a visual, it would look like the homes of people on the popular show *Hoarders*. You know, things constantly added; nothing removed. I contrasted this visual with the clean spare

lines of Shaker furniture. It looks so effortless, but it's so difficult to achieve. Using this furniture as a model, I handed out envelopes and invited participants to write out the core principles of their writing program. The stipulation was that it had to *fit* on the envelope. What follows is my list, now annotated, which I invite you to test for plausibility. Or you can create your own, which, I suspect, will be at least as good.

Choice

We often refer to reading and writing as skills, available for any task. But if they are skills, they are highly specific ones. Both are highly dependent on *prior knowledge* (a term that deserves its own chapter). As readers, we can be flummoxed by a text that presumes knowledge and vocabulary we don't possess; we feel comprehension slipping between our fingers. Even so, our reading capacity is far broader than our writing capacity, which is severely circumscribed by what we know and can reliably form opinions about. I can, reluctantly, read an essay on the Federal Reserve, but I can't write one.

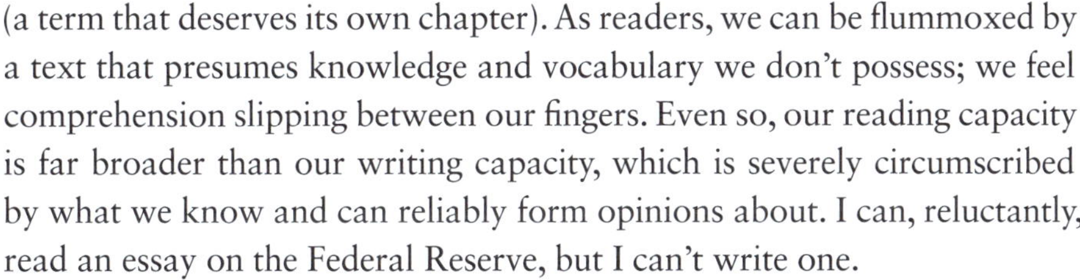

It follows that choice is critical for writing. A first condition is that writers can locate themselves in the topic, that they possess information, a point of view—that they can form an intention. Even so, when we give students choice, they often respond, "I don't have anything to write about." My immediate, but suppressed, reply is to just say, "Sure you do; every day something happens that you want to share with friends and family. There is something that annoyed you. Something that was pleasurable. Write about that!" Of course, that doesn't work: they need a way to access memory.

Inexperienced writers need to develop the capacity to inventory their lives and opinions, to mine them for material—indeed, to see their lives as writable. Choice is part of it—teachers not boxing writers into an unfamiliar topic, a rigid form, even a vocabulary. But they also need to assume what Liz Prather (2022) calls a writerly identity: the belief that they come to any writing funded with life experience that can be used. Listing—that original use of writing—is one of our best tools, with our best ideas rarely the first ones we write down.

They also need to believe that even when a topic is assigned, they can make it their own. They can find something in their autobiographic sense of self to draw on. Eleventh grader Eve describes taking this writerly approach when she was assigned one of the most unpromising of assignments, a process paper on how to make or do something:

> I thought, this is going to be terrible. This is going to be "How to Make a Sandwich"—and that's what the other kids did. I cannot do that. I cannot spend hours of my life writing about how to make a sandwich. So what I did, as soon as we were assigned it, I remember getting out of my chair and going up to my English teacher—I loved my English teacher, by the way—and I asked her, "Could I do an informative paper on 'How to Be Eve'?" And she goes, "As long as you have what's required."
>
> So I wrote it, "How to Be Eve." How to dress like Eve, how to act like Eve, and I actually made the intro very funny, "If you're having a midlife crisis or need a Halloween costume, then becoming Eve is just for you." It was funny like that. When we did peer review, I showed it to about four people, and they were laughing and showing it to their friends. (in Newkirk 2021, 32)

In this most constrained space, she persisted in making a choice.

Models and Demonstrations

I began this chapter with one of Don Murray's most provocative quotes: "Process cannot be inferred from product any more than a pig can be inferred from a sausage." This quote was the subject of considerable debate among those of us who worked with him because it seems to argue that knowledge of final products (what we read) is not useful in the process. At the time, I agreed that we can't infer the whole pig, but examining the sausage tells us something about sausage making. The final product doesn't teach us the process that produced it—but it does illustrate an end point we can aim for. If we read op-ed pieces regularly, we build intuitions about how they work. The trouble comes when writing in forms we haven't read.

Much of this learning—when we are immersed in texts of all kinds—is tacit, below the level of consciousness. We use this knowledge but can't name it. But there is a central role for a more explicit process of reading like a writer. Texts can serve as mentors, illustrating options for writers. Any piece of writing is the product of innumerable decisions that we can infer through a slowed-down process of reading. Take one of my favorite essay openings, from Dagoberto Gilb's essay "Victoria":

> I'll even blame the heat for my inability to remember which year it was—1986, give or take. It was hot like never before, my skin so porous it was hard to distinguish what side of it I was on. Like I could sweat and become a puddle. A dirty puddle because I'd absorbed that construction site. (1999, 105)

> Texts can serve as mentors, illustrating options for writers. Any piece of writing is the product of innumerable decisions that can be inferred through a slowed-down process of reading.

I love the colloquial rant-like feeling this opening gives. We enter, it seems, in the middle of it, and the narrator is inventing as he goes, like it was so damn hot that it couldn't be described; it wasn't enough to see himself as a puddle—it would be a dirty puddle. And this is just the beginning; he hasn't gotten to the smog yet. So for writers, here's an option: to break some rules for complete sentences and go on an associative rant, exaggerations welcome.

Without a sense of options, the very concept of choice is pretty meaningless. But students can mine texts that appeal to them for techniques, genre features, writerly moves, experiments (such as Gilb's) in voice. Working inductively, or as Katie Ray (1999) says, *descriptively*, we can name possibilities we can take over into our writing. And in the process, we can show how writers often intentionally break the rules we have been taught. Some of them make no sense at all, like we can't split an infinitive.

We're taught it's an error to actually do that (though I just did it). Why? Because you can't do that in Latin, where the infinitive is one word.

As teachers we can also be models; we can write with students, reveal our processes, and share what we produce. I asked eighth-grade teacher Mark Holt-Shannon what would be on his teaching highlight reel, and after some hesitation, he said:

> I think I'm good at modeling. And I think one of the things that gets a lot of kids is my enthusiasm about using writing to dig and dig and dig and discover something new and say it in a way that sounds great. I'm in the trenches. I'm doing this too—sometimes it's hard, and sometimes it pays off if you keep digging. (in Newkirk 2021, 93)

In my own classes, I didn't do the major assignments, but I always wrote with my students on the writing prompts that we used at the beginning of class.

One that I used early on was to have students write about their names—how they got their names, whether they liked them, how they morphed into nicknames. I told the story of getting the name Tom. When I was about ten, I asked my dad about this, assuming it had to do with the famous Toms I knew of (Jefferson, Edison, Paine). "No," he said. "None of those. I named you after the fool in *King Lear*." OK, it was a few years before I read the play and discovered that Tom the Fool only *acted* the fool.

I loved this shared writing time, how things would settle into quiet activity. I loved the sharing at the end, and I felt that even though this writing was one draft, to a prompt that they hadn't prepared for, it was often better, looser, improvisational, just more interesting than the more formal paper writing they did. It's the same experience I have when I look at the sketches that oil painters make in preparation for a big project. I often like these sketches better—the final painting feels just "thicker" in comparison.

The importance of teachers practicing writing themselves can't be overstated. Most teachers working in English and the language arts feel confident as readers. But the writing they did in college was primarily academic papers, rarely memoir or essay writing, and almost never fiction or poetry writing. In other words, none of us has had much experience with the kinds of writing that have the potential to engage student writers.

But the National Writing Project and similar programs for teachers, such as the one I directed, put teacher writing at the center, every day. Often, for the first time, participants could feel—really feel—what writing could be, how they could tap their experiences and say something meaningful for themselves and their readers. Without that embodied sense of being a writer, we can teach only as outsiders.

When teachers write, I believe there is a latency principle at work. While they experience the struggle of writing and the times when things don't go well, to a surprising degree, they write better than they expected. They surprise themselves and me, the instructor. I'd like to take some credit for this success, but on reflection I feel that they are reaping the benefit of a lifetime of reading. At a level maybe below consciousness, they know how writing works. They can also call on a lifetime of oral storytelling, what Mark calls "basking in that feeling of a well-told story" (Newkirk 2021, 93). They've been primed for the moment, ready, and for all the talk about struggle and pain, the feeling that comes at the end of a writing program is one of pure celebration, some of the most moving moments in my career.

Without that embodied sense of being a writer, we can only teach as outsiders.

Practice

It is difficult to even compose a section on the value of practice. It is one of those self-evident truths—to become competent at anything, you have to work at it. It's nonsensical to frame an argument against it. As Malcolm Gladwell shows in his book *Outliers* (2011), even those we rightly call geniuses (Mozart, the Beatles) put in hours of apprenticeship; he reckons ten thousand of them. When we are having surgery, we want a doctor who has performed the operation many times. We build stamina as a reader by reading voluminously. If we are looking for the reason students struggle with writing, we don't have to look far—they don't write enough, particularly if they find themselves in the lower academic tracks. Mina Shaughnessy, in the classic study of basic writers, estimates that many of them write less than a thousand words *in an entire school year* (1977).

The writing process is not simply something the writer does; it is something the writer owns. It is a regular and definable set of habits, practices, and attitudes that enables them to compose a text. These vary from writer to writer, dramatically. For example, my friend Jeffrey Wilhelm gathers material for a book and then drafts it in a two-week period, in twelve-hour days punctuated by eating, coffee, and short rides on his mountain bike. He then sends it to his cowriter Michael Smith, and this very rough draft is perfected in a back-and-forth series of exchanges. By contrast, I work in daily 90- to 120-minute sessions where I set a goal of five hundred words, and since I never learned to share in elementary school, I don't have a cowriter. While the processes differ, both are regular, often obsessively so.

In order to own a process, you need to write frequently, experiment, and find what works for you. Peter Johnston calls this a sense of "agency"—that whatever writing task we face, we have a process to accomplish it; indeed, we have a *history* of doing that. But if writing time is irregular and infrequent, the students have no basis for defining and owning a process, and any success they might have, a good grade, for example, is a kind of accident, even a surprise.

A number of teaching implications flow from this principle. Obviously the need to give writing a real place in the curriculum. Time, always time. I would argue that it means a shift to seeing writing as a studio course, more similar to an art class, than a traditional English or language arts class (Keene 2022). There is a place for teacher instruction, but teacher talk should not dominate as it often does. The focus should be on composing, with a classroom environment that supports reading and writing—and allows time for students to do both.

This runs counter to an entrenched image of what teaching is. In my second year of teaching at a high school in the Roxbury section of Boston, I had worked hard to use our book budget to replace the ponderous anthologies with real books that students might read. And on one day it was working; there was the wonderful feeling of engagement, each student with a book of choice—really reading. My principal came by at that point and said, so the whole class could hear, "Mr. Newkirk, will you please teach!"

Response

Writing naturally creates the anxiety of exposure. As an example, Sondra Perl tells the story of how one National Writing Project site, modeled after the Bay Area site, was established in New York City in 1978. She and her colleagues agreed that teachers needed to write—but sharing their writing in response groups? To them that seemed a bit too far, too "California," like sitting in hot tubs and exposing feelings. New Yorkers, they felt, wouldn't be willing to be so open. When they expressed their reservations to Jim Gray, national director, his response was simple: "If you want to run a Writing Project, you *will* have writing groups" (Perl 2015). They complied and, much to their great surprise, loved the results and never looked back.

A not so obvious question is What are we responding to when we confer with students? The writer? The writing? Both? In his second, totally revised edition of *A Writer Teaches Writing* (1984), Donald Murray argued that we respond to the student's response to their own writing. This sounds convoluted, but it makes sense. The writer has the responsibility of indicating where they are in the process of writing: what's going well, what they are trying to do, what they are struggling with, how a teacher can help. It's the same with any help-seeking situation; we indicate what help we need. Linda Rief, who learned from Murray, put it this way:

> You're there as a co-conspirator—"Teach me what you can teach me about this piece of writing. Tell me where you want to go with this, and let's see if I can help you get there." We can't know every single nuance of who these kids are as writers and readers unless we can sit beside them and

> get to their intent. I don't know how else you can get there. (Newkirk 2021, 119–20)

In asking writers, "Tell me where you want to go with this," Linda is inviting what Murray calls an "other self" to speak. "Eventually the other self learns to monitor the always changing relationship between where the writer is and where the writer intended to go" (Murray 1982, 166). Now clearly, inexperienced writers may need models and language to do this monitoring, and the model of the teacher is crucial. In my experience there are two foundational questions a writer must ask:

1. What am I trying to do? **Focus**
2. What material (details, stories, evidence, etc.) will help me do it? **Elaboration**

Inexperienced writers are usually underwriters—the events they want to portray are clear to them, but they underestimate the detail the reader will need to experience them. So a lot of my work is encouraging them to talk through some of the key places to discover what they could add. I believe that the more I ask them to expand in this way, the more able they will be to prompt themselves in the future. I also try to use what Peter Elbow (1973) calls "movies" of my reading; I phrase my comments to describe my experience of reading. I might say, "In the scene with your grandfather, I wondered how you were reacting to what he was telling you. Could you say something about that?"

In my own responding there is a clear bias toward being positive. In part, this is to counter the traditions of noting errors in writing (we still describe teacher responses as "correcting"). But writing, I feel, has a built-in sense of vulnerability, and writers have a tendency toward self-bullying, as high school teacher Liz Prather describes:

> We'll be out in the hall having a conference. And they'll just be giving themselves hell. They'll just be beating themselves up. And I will say, "Would you ever say this, what you're saying right now to yourself, to anybody else in our writing community? Would you say this to Evelyn, or to Erica, or Logan? Would you say this?"

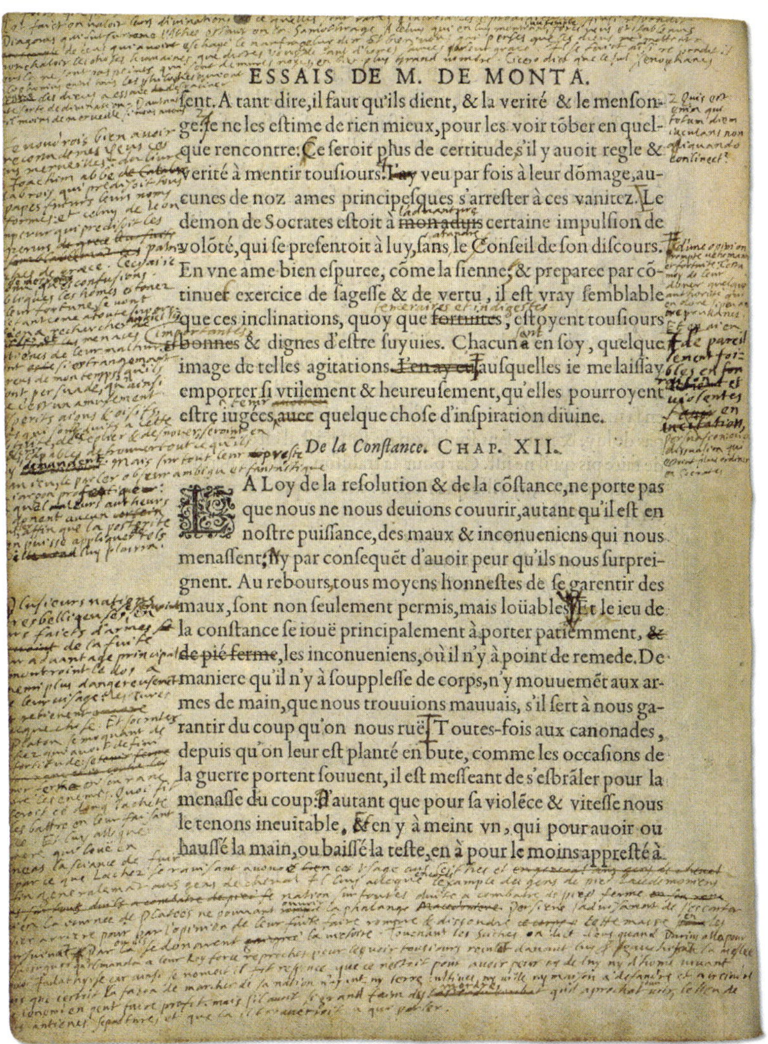

ESSAIS DE M. DE MONTA.

ſent. A tant dire, il faut qu'ils dient, & la verité & le menſonge: Je ne les eſtime de rien mieux, pour les voir tõber en quelque rencontre: Ce ſeroit plus de certitude, s'il y auoit regle & verité à mentir touſiours. I'ay veu par fois à leur dõmage, aucunes de noz ames principeſques s'arreſter à ces vanitez. Le demon de Socrates eſtoit à mon aduis certaine impulſion de volõté, qui ſe preſentoit à luy, ſans le Conſeil de ſon diſcours. En vne ame bien eſpurée, cõme la ſienne, & preparée par cõtinuel exercice de ſageſſe & de vertu, il eſt vray ſemblable que ces inclinations, quoy que fortuites, eſtoyent touſiours bonnes & dignes d'eſtre ſuyuies. Chacun a en ſoy, quelque image de telles agitations. I'en ay eu auſquelles ie me laiſſay emporter ſi vtilement & heureuſement, qu'elles pourroyent eſtre iugées auec quelque choſe d'inſpiration diuine.

De la Conſtance. CHAP. XII.

LA Loy de la reſolution & de la cõſtance, ne porte pas que nous ne nous deuions couurir, autant qu'il eſt en noſtre puiſſance, des maux & inconueniens qui nous menaſſent; ny par conſequẽt d'auoir peur qu'ils nous ſurpreignent. Au rebours, tous moyens honneſtes de ſe garentir des maux, ſont non ſeulement permis, mais loüables. Et le ieu de la conſtance ſe ioüe principalement à porter patiemment, & de pié ferme, les inconueniens, où il n'y à point de remede. De maniere qu'il n'y à ſoupleſſe de corps, n'y mouuemẽt aux armes de main, que nous trouuions mauuais, s'il ſert à nous garantir du coup qu'on nous ruë. Toutes-fois aux canonades, depuis qu'on leur eſt planté en bute, comme les occaſions de la guerre portent ſouuent, il eſt meſſeant de s'eſbrãler pour la menaſſe du coup: d'autant que pour ſa violẽce & viteſſe nous le tenons ineuitable, & en y à meint vn, qui pour auoir ou hauſſé la main, ou baiſſé la teſte, en à pour le moins appreſté à

Selective Revision, Montaigne Style

Beginning writers often fail to include details or information that readers need. Typically, on a first draft, they need to expand parts. To encourage them to do this, I borrow a technique from Montaigne, the inventor of the essay. His essays appeared on giant pages with big margins. Near the end of his life, he expanded his essays by extensive writing in the margins. So I ask students to print out the first draft of their essays on pages with big margins, two inches on both sides, find two or three places where they have more to say, and add it in the margins, as Montaigne did.

> And they would be horrified. They say, "No! Oh God, no. I would never say this."
>
> So my question is, "Why are you saying this to yourself? Why are you degrading yourself in this way?" (2022)

But it is so easy to imagine possible humiliation.

So . . . I am a countervoice, a positive one. One of my favorite things to do is to find an effective passage and read it aloud to the writer—read it *as literature*. I want them to hear it that way. Another strategy, again stolen from Peter Elbow, is pointing—identifying a memorable line, image, detail from a student's writing. In our writing institute for teachers, we would often end a week with a read-around and I would pass out slips of paper. After each person read, we all would describe, in a sentence or two, something specific that stayed with us. When it was over, participants gathered them like valentines. Collectively we are celebrating what we have all done, and celebration is a powerful form of response.

One of my favorite things to do is to find an effective passage and read it aloud to the writer—read it *as literature*.

A variation of pointing is snapping, with thumb and middle finger, a practice generally traced to readings of the Beat poets. It is a real-time response—similar to the call-and-response amen—used to show approval or liking, and it has become a convention of poetry slams.

Reflection

There's a story about a boy in a French school, run by a severe autocratic headmaster. One day on the playground this boy went up to the headmaster and asked, "Sir, when you sleep is your beard above or below the covers?" As might be expected, the headmaster reprimanded the boy for his "insolent" question. But a few days later, looking a bit haggard, he went up to the boy on the playground, and shook him, saying, "On account of you I have lost three nights' sleep."

Surely there are cases where self-consciousness can get in the way. And there are the myths that writing is an unexplainable visit from the Muses. But Murray never bought that mysticism: "writing is thinking, and a thinking act can, most of the time, be re-created in rational terms" (1982, 167).

In his book *The Writer's Mindset*, Chris Hall places great importance on teachers modeling this metacognition, including issues like

- where your idea came from and why it was important to write about
- parts you are excited about
- moves you are trying as a writer and why
- aspects of the piece that still need work or that you feel unsure about
- what you might try next (2021, 22)

The goal is to develop that other self—aware of writerly decisions and intentions.

In an interview with literacy expert Katie Ray, she said that the writing process was, in effect, the reflection that came retrospectively: "The writing process is the story you tell after you have written." In order to tell this story, she sees three conditions that need to be met:

1. You have to do enough writing, doing it regularly, to be aware of your own practice—of your work habits, choices, preferences, even the tools you like to use.
2. This frequency has to be coupled with a sense of agency, of being able to make decisions. If the writing is over-scaffolded, over-regulated, over-rubricked, with topic and process prescribed by the teacher, the student is merely following directions—a concern Katie has about the popular "gradual release of responsibility model" of teaching (Pearson and Gallagher 1983).
3. Reflection on this decision-making helps the writer stabilize a practice, an internally consistent approach to problem-solving: "I'm the kind of writer who when I write does this."

It reminds me of something Boston Celtics® great Kevin Garnett said when his number 5 was about to be raised to the roof of TD Garden. He thanked one of his early coaches, who taught him "not to be afraid to have a style."

Peter Johnston, in his classic book *Choice Words*, similarly places great importance on positioning the learner as a decision maker—building a personal history, a story in which the writer is the protagonist:

> The problem for us to solve, then, is how to arrange for children to tell many literary stories in which they are the successful protagonists? The heart of a good narrative is a character who encounters a problem and acting strategically solves it, usually (but not necessarily) attaining a goal. (2004, 31)

Stories like these help us work through difficulties; we can recall that we've been in similar situations before and worked our way through. We don't need to panic. We know that we have honed a process for making decisions, reducing big problems to a series of small ones, that will see us through. This is what resilience is all about.

DEMOCRACY

In the late 1970s Sondra Perl (1980) conducted groundbreaking research on the writing process, drawing on the psychotherapeutic work of Eugene Gendlin, particularly his concept of felt sense. Felt sense was an embodied, implicit, inchoate form of almost preknowing, which we tap into in the act of composing and make articulate. For example, we *sense* when we have a good topic to write about; it *feels* right to us. And sometimes in our writing we return to that sense to regain momentum. In her work with students and teachers, Perl developed guidelines, including listing and the generous use of silence (and waiting), to help them gain access to these latent possibilities to write.

Implicit in her work was, I felt, a strong connection to democratic values. Her graduate work, not coincidentally, was in the department at NYU that Louise Rosenblatt helped create. In an interview, I asked her directly about this connection:

> *The poet William Stafford said, "Writing is one of the last free human activities." To me that also equates with democracy. Something that is free, good, available to all. It's democratizing. It's not just for certain people or certain students. Writing is* there *and we just have to create situations where students can tap into it for themselves and discover it for themselves. Everyone has something to say.*

The role of the teacher is to create the conditions where it is safe enough so that students will say it to the people in the room:

> *Every voice in the room needs to be heard—whether it's a word, a line, a paragraph, an entire piece. It's bringing people's voices into the room, respecting those voices. It's listening to them openly, creating a dialogue among the ideas that populate the room. The job of the teacher is to listen really well. That's democracy at work.*

Perl added:

> *I feel as if that's all I've ever done.*

VOTE HERE
VOTE AQUÍ
在此投票
VEGAN
We're Not Nuggets

Chapter Five

TRANSLANGUAGING

Translanguaging: Proponents of translanguaging challenge the traditional view that languages are distinct, bounded entities. According to this traditional view, even when the language user is bilingual (or an emergent bilingual), they are operating exclusively in one language or the other, as if they are using distinct capacities of the brain. And historically, the aim of language education has been to wean the minoritized speaker from the first language so that they might learn English—even if this means prohibiting the use of any other language in schools. Translanguaging, by contrast, "focuses on . . . the unbounded dynamic and fluid use of multilinguals' entire linguistic repertoire" (García and Kleifgen 2019, 554). Translanguaging, then, is not a novel innovation in literacy instruction; rather, it honors the fluid and simultaneous nature of bilingual language use. It is the "communicative norm of bilingual communities" (García 2009, 51).

When I was a graduate student at the University of Texas, a story circulated about a debate in the Texas legislature. There was a move to appropriate money for teaching foreign language (that's what we called it then) in elementary schools. A number of legislators opposed this bill, and one memorably concluded his speech: "If English was good enough for Jesus, it's good enough for the children of Texas."

There is a long and painful history in this country of suppressing home languages so that children might be assimilated into mainstream culture—understood as Anglo-American and Christian (so called). Notoriously, Native children were forcibly sent to boarding schools, where they were prohibited from using their native language, leading to the extinction or near extinction of indigenous languages. A similar process of forced assimilation of First Nation peoples occurred in Canada. In states where there are large Latinx populations, particularly Arizona, there have been recent attempts to prohibit instruction in Spanish and to mandate large blocks of time that are English-only. And even before there were laws suppressing Spanish, the prohibition was there, as Gloria Anzaldúa recounts in "How to Tame a Wild Tongue":

> I remember being caught speaking Spanish at recess—that was good for three licks on the knuckles with a sharp ruler. I remember being sent to the corner of the classroom for "talking back" to the Anglo teacher when all I was trying to do was tell her how to pronounce my name. (1987, 53)

She reminds us: "So, if you want to really hurt me, talk badly about my language" (59).

The underlying fear—not at all hidden—is that the United States is inexorably moving toward becoming a pluralistic, multicultural country no longer dominated and controlled by a white, monolingual majority. And this is threatening to many. Even liberal historian Arthur Schlesinger Jr. railed against instruction in two languages: "Bilingualism shuts doors. It nourishes self-ghettoization, and ghettoization nourishes racial antagonism" (1991, 108). It leads, in his view, to social "fragmentation" and is a threat to the dream of "one people."

We could see translanguaging as utilizing a fund of knowledge—that the home language, the first language, of emergent bilingual students is not an impediment but an asset that we can leverage to assist the learning of English. But to reimagine the way we might use the home language, proponents of translanguaging ask us to rethink commonsense understandings of language itself. The very names—Spanish, English, Arabic, Chinese—in their singular form suggest bounded languages, often tied to a colonial past, each with their distinct grammars, vocabularies, and countries of origin. This is called monolingualism. However, in actual use, these boundaries break down, vocabulary is appropriated, and hybrids (Chinglish, Spanglish, regional variations) are created and re-created. Anzaldúa writes, "Change, evolución, enriquecimiento de palabras nuevas por invención o adopción" (1987, 55) is the nature of language development that adapts to and supports a way of life ("modo de vivir").

Bilinguals often will shift in midsentence from one language to another, "simultaneously using linguistic tools, knowledge, and features from all their languages," adjusting them for the purpose and audience (Fu, Hadjioannou, and Zhou 2019, 6). This process is sometimes called code-switching. But even that term succumbs to a monolingual viewpoint, suggesting two distinct competencies, two mental entities, that the speaker is switching to and from. Proponents of translanguaging stress that they are defining a single system, not the shuttling back and forth between distinct systems. Bilinguals and multilinguals possess a *repertoire*, a set of options that are present, available to use. Fu describes her own situation:

> The concept of translanguaging also helps me understand myself as a Chinese American, which is my integrated identity. It is hard for me to say how much of me is Chinese and how much American, but those two aspects of my cultural identity are inextricably intertwined in me as a whole, single being. . . . And even when an aspect is not readily visible in my behavior, it is still always there, informing my decisions, my actions, and my understanding of events and situations. (Fu, Hadjioannou, and Zhou 2019, 8)

She adds, "I still rarely dream only in English or Chinese" (8).

Carla España, coauthor of the magnificent guide for teaching Latinx students *En Communidad* (España and Herrera 2020), describes a similar fluidity. She notes in her formal schooling there were firm, separate spaces for Spanish and English use. But in her outside-of-school experiences she took advantage of her full repertoire of literacies, her "full self":

> As a bilingual speaker, this meant that growing up, I moved fluidly, using features of Spanish and English. There was no distinct "Spanish" and "English." In other words, I pulled from a language repertoire that had regional varieties of Spanish (from Valparaíso and Viña del Mar to Queens and El Barrio in New York City) and English (from Queens to Harlem and the Bronx in New York City). (13)

As she suggests, even the names we give to languages (English, Spanish) fool us into seeing firm boundaries. But *in use*, no such boundaries exist.

A rough comparison might be made to the game of tennis. It is possible to describe the baseline game and the game at the net. We can distinguish different skills needed for both. But these two games exist in a unified game, where options for baseline play and net play are always in the mind of the player. Certain situations—a short serve, a drop shot—invite the player to take the net. A player's sharply angled baseline shot can set up a move to the net, in anticipation of a difficult return where the opponent must stretch to make the shot. It's not simply a matter of having both games but of knowing the situations in which to shift—and doing so decisively. In the end, it is one game.

ENGLISH-ONLY

At one level, English-only rules make sense. We want students to be citizens and full participants in a society that is primarily English speaking and English writing. Employment opportunities are limited for those not fluent in English (though bilingualism is a big advantage). Why *not* place students in large blocks of time where they must participate in English? Why allow students to fall back on their home language?

Danling Fu, a leading proponent of translanguaging (and a key informant for this chapter) accepted this logic when in the 1990s she worked as an ESL consultant in New York City's Chinatown schools. She reasoned that most of the students in the schools where she was working were surrounded by Chinese—in their homes, in stores where they shopped, in food stands, in talk with their peers. School was the only place where they had sustained exposure to English, so why not restrict classes to English?

As she candidly admitted—it didn't work out.

Students went silent. And if we put ourselves in the position of those students, perhaps recalling our own struggles to learn a new language, this silence makes sense. In these large New York City classrooms, we can assume a great deal of instruction was whole-class teaching—a good deal of teacher talk, with hand raising to answer teacher questions. For one thing, following a native speaker for any length of time is exhausting, simply because of the speed at which they talk. At times it just seems a blur of language, without distinct words.

The other big problem was the mode of participation—the recitation model. The student who may naturally stumble or struggle with an answer has to do so in front of thirty other students. This "learning through public mistakes" (Philips 1972, 381) is understandably a flawed strategy that leads to silencing. Even if a student wants to enter into the flow of recitation, timing (and speed) is a problem. It takes time to process the question and formulate an answer, and by the time this has been done, the moment is gone. "Participating in multi-personal conversations can be one of the most challenging types of interactions, even for people with a high degree of proficiency in a language" (Fu, Hadjioannou, and Zhou 2019, 36). In a conversation with me, Danling admitted that to this day, she—an author of numerous books in English and frequent speaker at conferences—has trouble participating in faculty meetings.

The silent student, tuned out, overwhelmed by the onrush of English, takes on a look that I think all teachers see at times (and not simply from English language learners). It is a blank look, unresponsive to what is going on, still, tired; often the head goes down on the desk. Or there is some form of activity—doodling, peeling the paint off a pencil, chewing an eraser, writing on a desk (or their hand)—some form of life and distraction. It is a look that suggests no cognitive activity, that, to put it unkindly, looks stupid. Christina Ortmeier-Hooper, author of *The ELL Writer* (2013), describes her own sensation of the heavy feeling of being stupid in a German immersion class, of feeling stripped of all that made her an intelligent, knowledgeable person. This, I suspect, is what happens in the sink-or-swim English-only classroom.

English-only runs counter to a broader learning principle—namely, using a stronger representational system to help, to bootstrap, the learning of a newer and less familiar system. An analogy can be made to young children learning to write. For many, drawing is a stronger system; for some, even before they can write full sentences they can create elaborate and detailed drawings, often inventing ways to show action. At age six my daughter drew a "happy puppy machine" showing the stages of the creation of happy puppies.

Unfortunately, schools often move very quickly to lined paper that increasingly restricts the space for drawing and perceive the drawing itself as pulling students away from learning to write. The systems compete. So like English-only, you have print-only—pulling the learner away from the stronger system.

An alternative would be to piggyback the new learning on the stronger existing system; in the case of young drawers, to show they can use writing to form captions to their drawing, represent talk in speech bubbles, or represent thinking in thought bubbles—all the while maintaining the options to draw. Writing is not restricted to a single mode of representation; modes interact. By using the drawing as a resource, we can celebrate the strengths the students bring to composing, and these young drawers can become known for their skills.

Similarly, if we view competency in the home language as a resource, we can use it to leverage English learning. For example, Fu and her colleagues present a vignette where Rosa, a fourth grader who has been in the United States for a year and a half, tries to find her way into a lesson on animals. As it turns out, Rosa has a lot she could bring in, as her grandmother owns a farm and Rosa has assisted her in the birth of a calf and she is very proud of being part of that ordeal (Fu, Hadjioannou, and Zhou 2019, 32)—something that would surely be of interest to her peers. But she cannot translate this into English quickly enough to participate in the rapid flow of classroom recitation. She quickly becomes overwhelmed by the pace of discussion, and her story is never shared, her expertise never acknowledged. In the end, she puts her head on her desk and stops listening. If she had been given an option to use some of her Spanish, maybe writing an account in a mix of Spanish and English and sharing it, using Spanish names when she didn't have the English ones, she could have been a participant, a player.

Writing is not restricted to a single mode of representation; modes interact. By using the drawing as a resource, we can celebrate the strengths the students bring to composing, and these young drawers can become known for their skills.

In his long and distinguished career, Canadian researcher Jim Cummins has dismantled the key assumptions of English-only: namely that attention to the home language interferes with the learning of English or that the systems of learning the first language (L1) and the second (L2) are fundamentally separate. By contrast, he proposes the concept of "common underlying proficiency" (2000). Proficiency, oral and written, in L1 can support—not detract from—learning English or another second language. L1 proficiency is an asset, not a confusing complication or distraction:

> In short, the research data clearly show that within a bilingual program, instructional time can be focused on developing students' literacy skills in their primary language without adverse effects on the development of their literacy skills in English. (2000, 39)

Enhanced L1 proficiency "can provide a conceptual foundation for long-term growth in English" (39). This in addition to the social-emotional benefits of staying connected to familial culture and ethnic identity made possible by first-language literacy.

In effect, Cummins provides a conceptual and research base for translanguaging, a concept he strongly supports: "When promoted together, two languages enrich each other rather than subtracting from each other" (2000, 28).

English language learners who were excellent students in their home countries, and often models of diligent behavior, find themselves in an environment of low expectations and are often foreclosed from entering honors or AP courses later in their school career.

Another impediment to the emergent bilingual has to do with the tracking system that often begins in late middle school. It is hardly a secret that rigid tracking systems are stable—once you are in a track, you stay there (Oakes 2005). Nor that schools often use them to segregate students perceived as unmotivated and behavior problems, fairly or not. Another characteristic is that students in these lower tracks often do less sustained writing or reading and more fill-in-the-blank worksheet work. English language learners who were excellent students in their home countries, and often models of diligent behavior, find themselves in an environment of low expectations and are often foreclosed from entering honors or AP courses later in their school career. Schools disregard their strength in their L1 literacy and undermine their identity as strong students (Ortmeier-Hooper 2013).

IDENTITY

Schooling—by its very nature—involves a separation from the home. It is a testament to the belief that the home is not fully sufficient to educate children and to create a *public*. The school bus arrives, children get on, parents may wave, and the ritual of separation is complete. For some of the children on the bus, the rituals of school will seem no more than a continuation of home practices, as Shirley Heath documented in her profound study *Ways with Words* (1983). Speech patterns such as display questions, where the teacher asks questions for which she obviously knows the answer ("How does a duck sound?"), are familiar. For other students on the bus, particularly some children of color and children whose home language is not English, the separation is more radical and alienating (Delpit 2006). It can feel like the cost of education, of assimilation, is an abandonment of a primary identity and language.

In his elegant memoir, *Hunger of Memory*, Richard Rodriguez (1983) tells his own story of separation. He comes to identify with values of school, becoming a "good student," but in the process loses connection with family and his home language. In fact, he becomes embarrassed by his parents and their inability to understand his need to be alone to read.

To all outward appearances, the "scholarship boy" is a success—but psychologically he is stranded between two worlds, no longer a member of his home culture but not really a member of the educated community he aspires to. He often feels like an outsider there, too, an imposter, who can expose himself at any moment with the trace of an accent or a lapse in social knowledge. Rodriguez describes a powerful longing to reconnect, to reexperience the intimacy of his home culture.

In deeply emotional testimony during her confirmation hearing, Judge Ketanji Brown Jackson described the desolate loneliness of her first months of undergraduate school at Harvard. Here she had reached the pinnacle of the American educational system—and she was miserable:

> "I'm from Miami, Florida," she said. "Boston is very cold. It was—it was rough. It was different from anything I'd known. There were lots of students who were prep school kids, like my husband, who knew all about Harvard. And that was not me. And I think the first semester I was really homesick. I was really questioning, 'Do I belong here? Can I make it in this environment?'
>
> "And I was walking through the yard in the evening and a Black woman I did not know was passing me on the sidewalk," Jackson continued. "And she looked at me. And I

> guess she knew how I was feeling, and she leaned over as we crossed and said, 'Persevere.'" (Dwyer 2022)

Education like this exacts a price, entails a loss.

In her book *Cultivating Genius: An Equity Framework of Culturally and Historically Responsive Literacy*, Gholdy Muhammad (2020) makes identity a pillar of instruction. She describes how when she works with teachers, she takes pictures, and when she shares them, participants look to find themselves. Students, she claims, are doing the same thing when they enter a classroom: "They are looking for themselves. They are seeking to find curriculum and instructional practices that honor the multiple aspects of who they are" (69).

She describes a series of activities, like telling the story of your name, that honor their identity and roots. There is also a rich literature on names, sometimes dissatisfaction with names, most notably Sandra Cisneros' section of *The House on Mango Street* where Esperanza says she would prefer "Lisandra or Maritza or Zeze the X" (1983). "Unforgettable," a widely watched Poetry Slam video, featuring Pages Matam, Elizabeth Acevedo, and G. (George) Yamazawa (2014), builds on the same theme, as each laments being given an Anglo name that doesn't fit them, for example, George, the name of "some old dead white guy."

Other common activities are writing their own versions of George Ella Lyon's well-known poem "Where I'm From" (n.d.). Some teachers diversify the mentor text by including versions from different ethnicities—such as Lina Abojaradeh's, a Palestinian Jordanian "artivist," whose video poem "I Am Limitless" (2017) combines images and text. Another option is to invite students to create an "identity map" (Ortmeier-Hooper 2013), a visual representation of important aspects of their histories, aspirations, passions, accomplishments—including lists, arrows, photographs, drawings, timelines. This map (to mix metaphors) can be a seedbed for a range of topics for reading and writing.

I can think of no form of alienation more powerful—no greater assault to identity—than being cut off from one's first language, the language of one's first words, of food, of family stories, names, places. For emergent bilinguals, this first language can be an invaluable tool in learning English, but even for language learners proficient in English, translanguaging can help maintain a connection to one's home language. For example, teachers can identify mentor texts that model strategies for bringing L1 into their writing in English, as Junot Díaz famously does in his novels and short stories and Yamile Saied Méndez (2020) does in her novel *Furia*. Teachers can encourage students to try out these techniques, for example, bringing L1 dialogue into a literacy narrative or short story.

Students also need access to texts in both Spanish and English; this is a central theme of Carla España and Luz Yadira Herrara's *En Comunidad* (2020). The aim is to "encourage students either to hear one language and read the words in another, or hear more than one language in one text" (50). Even their own writing intersperses Spanish expressions, often untranslated. This pairing of languages is particularly effective with poetry and children's books that we can easily place side by side and compare. They offer a wealth of possibilities from Sandra Cisneros, Francisco Alarcón, Matt de la Peña, and many others. There are also online suggestions including the Latino Book Review's (2017) recommendation of ten contemporary poets whose work appears in Spanish and in English.

FOUR STRATEGIES

The teaching options—and challenges—in incorporating translanguaging are far too complex to be dealt with in any detail here. But it's possible to suggest four basic options for the writing of bilinguals and emergent bilinguals.

Substitution

If students have strong writing skills in L1, they might begin by substituting known English words and phrases in the L1 writing—creating a mixed-language text. As the writing proficiency in English increases, more of the writing will be in English. The student might begin by substituting English into L1 and then later move to substituting L1 into

English. Danling Fu encouraged teachers in Chinatown to allow mixed usage of two languages in writing (2007, 228). She noted that this language mixing naturally occurs when English terms, like *flea market*, have no easy Chinese equivalent and represent students' life experience in this country. The opportunity to write in L1 is important because it allows the student to better represent an understanding of the academic topic.

This might be understood as an example of the principle of focus in learning—that we should avoid multiplying the challenges the learner faces. For example, it is a truism in language instruction that when introducing new vocabulary, you keep to familiar syntax—and the reverse: when introducing new sentence constructions, you stay with familiar vocabulary. In the case of a history lesson on the differences between the Revolutionary and Civil Wars, this information is new and unfamiliar, a challenge to be sure. But we complicate that challenge—and fail to gauge student learning—if we require students to represent that learning in a written language they are also struggling to learn.

An obvious challenge for the teacher unfamiliar with a student's L1 is reading and evaluating this writing. But in my discussions with teachers, this has not been a major stumbling block. There are often possible interpreters in the class or teaching staff; the student might also be able to orally explain in English the gist of what they've written or write a short summary in English.

As students transition to English writing, Danling advises tolerance of "broken English"; in fact, she sees it as inevitable because of the syntactic difference between Chinese and English. It was common for students in Chinatown to write, "I eight o'clock go to school," and it frustrated teachers. But this was only using the Chinese syntax for English sentences: she noted that in Chinese, everything is between the subject and the verb. In English, it is SVO (subject-verb-object); in Chinese it is S . . . V . . . O. If both languages are in play, she explains, students can develop the metalinguistic awareness of differences, and teachers can understand the logic (and necessity) of errors.

Translation

Probably the most obvious form of translanguaging is translation. It might involve gathering information in L1 and translating it into English, a process that often has multiple levels. Take, for example, Phoenix middle school teacher Ginette Rossi's assignment to gather family recipes to create a recipe book. She provides the assignment in English, but to interview a family member (a *tía* or an *abuela*) in Spanish, students have to translate the questions themselves. Then they must translate the answers back into English. Moreover, there are familiar terms for amounts for pinch (*pizca*) or handful (*puñado*) that they need to translate into conventional amounts.

And sometimes there are further steps, a process called double washing. On an assignment involving family interviews on the American dream (Fernandes, Clark-Barnes, and Ortmeier-Hooper 2022, 86), a student explained this process: from Chinese to basic English to "better English." It went from a basic translation, then a Google check for synonyms and work on grammar (the first wash), to a review by her writing group (the second wash), to the final revisions she made (the third wash). The authors argue that in an evaluation of this process, we should give students credit for these layers of translation and that it is unfair to use a standard rubric that simply looks at the end product.

The possibilities for translation are exponentially expanded with tools like Google Translate™—though they don't help everyone. As Danling pointed out to me, if there is a great disparity between the L1 and L2 writing abilities, the student probably can't read the translation. But translation tools allow writers to substitute L1 vocabulary in their English writing—and (*rápidamente*) quickly locate the needed term. They also allow monolingual teachers to access translations of L1 writing to better assess a student's understanding of material.

I admit that Google Translate was new to me, and I tried it out on the "English was good enough for Jesus" story that I began the chapter with. Here is part of what instantly came back:

> Varios legisladores se opusieron a este proyecto de ley, y uno concluyó su discurso de manera memorable: "Si el inglés fue lo suficientemente bueno para Jesús, es lo suficientemente bueno para los niños de Texas."

Besides a flush of vanity in seeing my words translated, it occurred to me that I had motivation to learn the Spanish in this translation, to pay special attention to vocabulary I *might want to use—discurso, niños, bueno, para.*

Some genres of writing are ideal for translation. In her book *Next Generation Genres: Teaching Writing for Civic and Academic Engagement*, Jessica Early (2022) identifies the public service announcement as a real-world type of writing that performs an important function. It is a real genre in a way that the generic persuasive paper is not. It is brief, highlighting important information—and designed to raise awareness, alter behavior, and often let disadvantaged pockets of a community be aware of opportunities. Often it is a language barrier that keeps this information from community members—so it is a natural form for presentation in multiple languages. Indeed, the writer-presenter who can manage this bilingual task is a community asset.

Even for emergent bilinguals writing in L1, there are opportunities to do some minimal translation work. For example, teachers might ask them to write in English a one- or two-sentence summary. They might have students title their writing in L1 and in English. They might teach kids to pull a key sentence and translate it into English. In other words, they can invite manageable acts of translation. Or, in conversation with the teacher, students might use conversational English to describe what they have written (obviously useful if the teacher is monolingual).

Transmediation

Transmediation is a fancy term for something that happens all the time. If we write a few lines and then read them aloud, we are transmediating; that is, we are shifting from a print medium to an oral medium. Or, we might illustrate the text with a photograph, adding a visual medium. Just as translanguaging rejects the firm boundaries of language, transmediation rejects the firm boundaries of media, which we are always intermixing, particularly as technology enables us to integrate sound, images, text, movement, typefaces, and more. From a learning perspective, we can use stronger media competences to bootstrap emergent ones: as already noted, this regularly happens with children's drawings supporting their writing.

Humans are profoundly visual—by some estimates, 30 percent of our cerebral cortex is involved with vision (Grady 1993). Babies can distinguish faces at around three months, and they recognize their mother's face considerably earlier than that. Young children often learn to draw well before they can form letters. And to say they learn does not mean they are taught. These visual capacities are natural just as speaking is natural—and these visual capacities transcend language barriers. Consequently, art, drawing, photography, and sculpture are extraordinarily useful in bridging language and cultural divides. When we work from vision, from color and forms and images and pictures, we are working from strength.

Just as translanguaging rejects the firm boundaries of language, transmediation rejects the firm boundaries of media, which we are always intermixing, particularly as technology enables us to integrate sound, images, text, movement, typefaces, and more.

Not surprisingly, then, visual representations can be enormously useful in bilingual education. Danling Fu describes some of these possibilities:

> In schools I have seen ELL adolescents enjoy drawing strings of pictures to tell about their lives in their home country, and contrast their past lives in villages with green hills and rice patties to their present lives in ghettos with garbage along the streets and iron bars on apartment windows. I have seen their published photo books with one word or a phrase captioning each page to express what they have learned during their field trips; and about their families and communities; and their observations of moon, clouds, and city bridges. (2007, 234)

The stronger system brings along the emergent system. The picture needs the caption. We can invite a fuller repertoire for representing meaning and understanding.

Strategic Mixing

Junot Díaz begins his autobiographical story "Drown" this way: "We were on our way to the colmado for an errand, a beer for my tía" (1996, 3). In this way he establishes a pattern of using some Spanish terms, untranslated, in his narrative.

He, of course, might have chosen to be more strictly monolingual; the sentence could have read: "We were on our way to the grocery store for an errand, a beer for my aunt." Same basic meaning, right? But his version feels more authentic, and appealing, even if we don't know the Spanish—we can infer what *colmado* means and probably know what *tía* means.

Díaz (and, of course, Anzaldúa) opened the way for writers to bring Spanish terms and expressions into their writing in English. It feels more true to experience to write, "Hola. ¿Cómo estás?" rather than the stiff translation, "Hi. How are you?" Of course, this pattern was used earlier with Yiddish by Jewish writers and comedians who might use, untranslated, terms like *schmutz* for dirt or filth. Some Yiddish words, like *glitch*, *schmaltz*, and *chutzpa*, have become part of everyday English.

In her novel *Furia*, a story of an Argentinian female soccer (no, *fútbol*) player, author Yamile Saied Méndez (2020) frequently shifts to Spanish terms and allows the context, or familiarity with English cognates, to create understanding. For example, the main character Camila ducks out of sight and buys cookies, to disguise the fact that she had discovered her father with a young woman:

> I couldn't stand in the middle of the sidewalk like this, so I darted to the kiosco across the street. From the display case, I grabbed a Capitán del Espacio alfojor. I hadn't seen this brand of chocolate cookie for years. (2020, 212)

Interestingly, an Arizona teacher I spoke to who wanted to use this book felt that it would be controversial (because of the Spanish insertions) to introduce it in an English class, so she did so in a Spanish class. The bias is that strong.

Even when students are writing predominantly in English, this subtle shifting should be an option, especially when writing about a home culture where the language is not English. The use of L1 terms—place-names, common expressions, product names—can help the reader feel a connection to that culture, even if it takes some guesswork to understand. And often there are not exact English equivalents; a *colmado* is not exactly a *grocery store*. *Hola* is not exactly *hi*. And some L1 words have an emotional resonance that the English "equivalent" does not possess: *tía* does not equal *aunt*.

WHO'S IN THE MINORITY?

Around 2000, Danling invited me to visit a New York school located in Spanish Harlem, so that I might see the work she was doing as a consultant. At one point this district was largely Puerto Rican but now it was more Mexican Harlem. One moment in that visit stands out in my mind. I was in a small group of middle schoolers, asking them about their reading and writing, and it became obvious that their proficiency in English varied significantly. One boy in particular seemed to hunker down and avoid eye contact. But a girl in the group brought him in, translating my questions into Spanish and his answers to English. Occasionally she used English words that she thought he would know. Back and forth, effortlessly.

At that moment, I felt my lack, my linguistic, monolingual limitations. Here I was a college professor, waterlogged with degrees and publications, and I was witnessing something I couldn't remotely do, the easy movement back and forth, language to language, mixing both at times. And it also occurred to me that she was more representative of English speakers than I was. That I was the minority. There are an estimated 1.5 billion English speakers in the world, and the vast majority learned it as a second (or third) language (Statista 2023). I was momentarily stunned by this collective global effort to learn English and my own incapacity to move outside of English, and I was embarrassed by the irritation I sometimes felt at understanding an accent, even though accents are the norm.

Proponents of translanguaging challenge us all to rethink the bounded ways in which we conceive language, thinking often rooted in ethnocentrism and nationalism. We are challenged to honor the fluid ways in which languages interact, the way they combine—*mestizo*, from the Latin *mixticius*. As Gloria Anzaldúa uses the term, it is not simply a racial designation but an attitude, an unwillingness to be bounded by language or culture, to continually walk from one to the other (1987, 79).

Chapter Six

STORY

Story: The story is a primary vehicle for explaining, entertaining, informing, socializing, and establishing an identity as an individual or community. It ranges in complexity from the joke and anecdote to the novel and epic. Stories typically have plots; that is, there is some initial conflict or tension—some trouble—that is brought to a conclusion in the telling. Psychologists claim that in terms of cognition, the story has "privileged status"—it is the primary and most appealing way in which we understand the world and ourselves (Willingham 2004). Consequently, it is not simply a literary form but a primary mode of understanding that has consequence for learning in all subjects and for forms of persuasion and explanation. It pervades all discourse.

To make a case for story as a major idea must appear as bold as making a case for breathing. I mean, Homer (pictured on previous page) and Dostoevsky hardly need me to provide some basis for their significance. ELA teachers hardly need to be convinced of the importance of novels and stories—it's why most of us *became* teachers. It is impossible to imagine social interactions without the attraction of storytelling. Our very identity is built on our life stories: as the poet Lisel Mueller once wrote, "the story of our life becomes our life" (1980). By extension, the story of our family becomes our family. The story of our nation becomes our nation—and we are surely fighting about which story needs to be told.

My aim in this chapter will be more modest. I'd like to argue that we regularly misconceive story as a *kind of writing*, often referred to as narrative—the two are often used interchangeably. Usually, narrative appears in some form of trinity of types, often with argumentation and exposition (or informational writing), with the implicit, or sometimes explicit, assumption that narrative is the easiest of the three and more appropriate for younger students. In the past, Piaget's concept of "formal operations" has been used to explain the greater abstractive demands of exposition and argumentation, a reason for the developmental appropriateness of placing them in the later grades (Lunsford 1979). I'd like to argue that these assumptions are at odds with cognitive research on narrative (its centrality in comprehension and memory), and practically, it leads to an unhealthy compartmentalization.

Fundamentally, the trinity—narrative, informational, argumentative—doesn't hold up as a category system. Yes, all category systems leak. But in this case they represent what philosophers call a category error, using conflicting principles to make distinctions. Imagine we were asked if we would like fruit or dessert. It makes no sense: fruit is a kind of food and dessert is the stage of a meal—two conflicting principles. The problem with the narrative-informational-argumentative trinity is not as obvious but it's essentially the same issue.

In his authoritative book of discourse, James Kinneavy (1971) makes a crucial distinction between the aims and the modes of discourse. The *aims* are the purposes or basic goals that we use language for; he defines them as literary, referential, persuasive, and expressive. In his view, all of these aims are present in any text or statement, but one predominates. *Modes*, on the other hand, refer to principles of thought that permit us to consider reality in a particular way; he names the basic modes as classification, narration, description, and evaluation. Clearly we use modes for all of the aims he defines; description is a tool for the historian, the biologist, and the poet.

The problem with the narrative-informational-argumentative trinity is that it mixes modes and aims. Narrative is clearly a mode—we don't have the aim to narrate; rather, we narrate for a purpose. Informational is clearly an aim where the focus is on "factuality," "comprehensiveness," and what Kinneavy (1971) calls "surprise value" (something unexpected and interesting). Argumentative discourse might be seen as a component of an aim, that of being persuasive, with a focus on logos, or logic. We can see the problem if we ask whether a popular nonfiction book, for example, *Evicted*, by Matthew Desmond (2017), is narrative or informational—we're back to the fruit-or-dessert problem. It's both. Narrative or argumentative? Again, both. This is not simply leakage; it's sloppy thinking.

So ingrained is this view of narrative as a type of writing that for the rest of this chapter, I'll invite you to simply do a thought experiment: What if we imagine narrative as the primary mode of all writing—that no matter the aim, we rely on narrative to make sense of what we read? It is home base. We rely on it to provide the motivation for all sustained reading. Even the most formal scientific reports, even technical proposals, have some kind of narrative arc. Moreover, when we feel completely separate from narrative, we usually lose interest, lose human contact, lose the forward motion of what is said or written. If we have any choice in the matter, we eventually stop reading. This is not evidence that we are lazy; it's evidence that we are human.

THE STORY, THE LIST, AND DEATH BY POWERPOINT®

If we look at the books of the Bible, we can easily group them into those that are primarily lists (e.g., Numbers, Leviticus, Proverbs, Psalms) and those that tell stories (Genesis, Exodus, Job, Revelations, the Gospels). Books like Deuteronomy are part narrative and part a list of laws. It is not a stretch to imagine that early in the development of writing systems, two millennia before the Christian era, our primary organizational forms had been created.

According to Jack Goody, author of *The Domestication of the Savage Mind* (1977), the first extended forms of writing were lists. He argues that the capacity to create lists, to pull language from the stream of talk and create categories and classification, was an enormous cognitive development. Not only did lists support increasingly complex governmental and business structures, but they also opened the way to systems of classification that form the basis of history and the sciences. In creating categories of information, the list invited the maker to abstract from individual facts or items and reflect on the organization of data. Lists can be almost endlessly subdivided—animals ultimately sorted into domain, kingdom, phylum, down to species and breed. They create repositories of information vastly more extensive (and accurate) than any human could possess. The list also enables efficient retrieval of information; the eye can move flexibly among columns and categories depending on our purpose, a process I call extractive reading.

The writing young children do mirrors this pattern of evolution; they often begin by writing labels and move to more conceptually defined lists (e.g., lists of family members, friends, even words they know). In writing about pets they might list features of the pet (e.g., name, breed, color, misbehavior), a form that has been called an attribute list. (At about age six one of our daughters made a list of everything in the house she wanted when my wife and I died—basically everything.) Even their early stories are really chronological lists (i.e., chronicles), often bed-to-bed stories that list events of the day in the order they happened. The shaped story, with conflict and resolution, is a later development (Newkirk 1987). In effect, six-year-olds recapitulate the early history of writing; they discover the utility of these fundamental writing forms, particularly the list.

According to Goody, the primary use of writing in the Assyrian period was bureaucratic and not literary—such as deeds, bills of sale, ledgers, and rental agreements. But there were later narrative uses as well, the best known being the epic *Gilgamesh*, written about 1200 BC, derived from tales and songs about a legendary Mesopotamian king. It is generally considered the first extended written fictional story. So, early in the development of writing systems, we have two powerful, protean forms of organization—the story and the list. One is temporal and episodic, the other nontemporal and classificatory. One requires sustained attention; the other is set up for opportunistic extraction of information.

It is probably inevitable that writing evolved this way because the story and the list correspond to the two memory systems that humans possess—episodic memory and semantic memory. Semantic memory corresponds to the classificatory possibilities of the list. *Apple* is part of a network of categories—it is a *fruit*, and there are many varieties of apples that vary in *sweetness* and *color*. It is used in *baking*, such as in turnovers, apple crisp, and, of course, pies. It grows on *trees*, usually growing about twenty feet tall, and the *wood* is often used for barbecue grilling. And so on ad infinitum. *Apple* can also call up memories, episodes—literary ones, like the Genesis story of Eve and the apple and the poisoned apples in *Snow White*. Or it can call up personal ones, like sneaking into an apple orchard to steal apples, losing a baby tooth in an apple, enjoying apple pie at Thanksgiving dinner. Cumulatively we construct these episodes into a narrative of our lives, a story we tell about ourselves.

For all their power, for all the control lists and categories give us, for all the amazing access we now have to information, lists are not designed for sustained reading. In fact, we are pretty ruthless when reading for information. Jakob Nielsen and Kara Pernice have performed elaborate eye-tracking studies to determine what parts of a webpage readers pay attention to. This is critically important information for web designers (Nielsen 2006). They created stunning images, like weather radar maps, showing the small areas that receive attention and the expanse that is ignored. They found that readers followed an F pattern—reading the title, then the first line, then moving down the page, taking in the beginning of the next couple of lines and ignoring the bottom half of the page. F is for *fast*. Any key information has to be in there early—no writing introductions.

Problems arise when readers are expected to sustain attention to a text or presentation that takes the form of a list. One of my colleagues once remarked, "We know a student is in trouble when they keep starting paragraphs with 'And another . . .'" I felt, literally felt, this problem when I served on our local school board. In each meeting there were several presentations, all PowerPoint. Sometimes they were artfully done, with clever use of images and text that appeared as the presenter scrolled down.

But the contents were one list after another, bullet points, aptly named, because they were deadly. Part of the issue was selectivity—a presentation of twenty slides with ten or more pieces of information per slide . . . well, you can do the math. My major problem, though, was the lack of any story or plot to connect the slides or to anchor the presentation in human experience. It was one damn thing after another. I wanted to interrupt and say, "Just tell me what a day is like! What does this look like in a classroom? Bring a kid into the picture!" Obviously, anecdotal stories are not representative, but without stories there was no possibility of engagement, and without a narrative arc it was hard—impossible—for me to stay tuned in and at times even to pretend to be tuned in.

But I would argue that extractive reading, mining texts for facts and quotes, contributes to confirmation bias. We fit this information into preexisting frames and beliefs, leading to the dogmatism and fragmentation we see so much of today.

STAY WITH ME—THE CHALLENGE OF SUSTAINED READING (AND WRITING)

Extractive reading is invaluable for daily life, and the internet has exponentially expanded our access—no fact seems unavailable. We've come a long way from the Renaissance reading wheel, which allowed consultation with a set of texts (see Figure 6.1). But I would argue that extractive reading, mining texts for facts and quotes, contributes to confirmation bias. We fit this information into preexisting frames and beliefs, leading to the dogmatism and fragmentation we see so much of today. To really change our thinking, we need sustained contact with something novel or foreign or uncomfortable. We need to undergo something. Sustained reading—following a train of thought, dwelling with a character, feeling a relationship with a writer or teller or narrator—brings the potential for change that the mere retrieval of fact does not. Sustained reading can open us to complexity and depth, to characters as intricate and interesting as Austen's Emma, Morrison's Pecola, Baldwin's Baldwin.

But what sustains us as readers? What keeps us moving? How do writers build a sense of continuity? I contend that writers who want to sustain the attention of readers must learn to use narrative tools.

Figure 6.1 *Renaissance Reading Wheel—a Kind of Search Engine*

To begin with, they must *narrate*. We struggle with texts that don't seem authored, when no one is home.

In *The Sense of Style* (2014), Steven Pinker describes the role of the narrator as a kind of guide: "The writer can see something that the reader has not yet noticed, and he orients the reader's gaze so that she can see it for herself" (28–29). The writer is not superior to the reader, just familiar with something the reader doesn't know about. The focus is on the specific—"people (or other animate beings) who move around in the world and interact with objects" (29). Even if the subject matter is abstract, the writer works to "show the events making up the subject matter transparently, by narrating an unfolding plot with real characters doing things, rather than by naming an abstract concept that encapsulates those events in a single word" (48–49). A characteristic of this style is cognitive energy, a palpable fascination with the material. And these narrators are solicitous—if the material is complex, they find a metaphor to help us out. If a concept is abstract, they find an example to pin it down for us. If things get too serious, they throw in some humor. We are cared for.

The presence of a narrator builds continuity, a sustaining presence. It's similar to teaching. I recall a conversation with a beginning teacher who felt his lessons were not well organized; one thing did not lead logically to another. His advisor reminded him that *he* himself—his personality, humor, manner of interacting, even appearance—helped create continuity and stability. (It's why substitutes who follow the lesson are disruptive.) The same could be said for a narrator; there is a sensibility, voice, attitude that a reader comes to expect and hopefully appreciate.

Peter Elbow (2012) reminds us that reading is a temporal act—we are moving through time as we read, and the challenge for any writer is to "bind time," to hold the attention of the reader through what Elbow calls "imbued energy." It is misleading, he argues, to think of structure as spatial forms—an outline, an inverted pyramid—that say nothing about *why* we voluntarily move forward. Organization is not a static form; we *experience* organization as an invitation to continue reading. He brilliantly describes how this happens:

> So where do writers find the energy that binds written words together so as to pull readers along from one part to the next and make them experience the text as a coherent whole? . . . Successful writers lead us on a journey to satisfaction by way of expectations, frustrations, half satisfactions and temporary satisfactions: a well-planned sequence of yearnings and reliefs, itches and scratches. (303)

The conventional forms we teach students fail to create any sense of a journey. Elbow calls the five-paragraph theme, as it is usually taught, an "anti-perplexity machine" (309). It focuses on a thesis and support with virtually no attention as to the problem the thesis is responding to. What is the need for this argument? What question is it resolving? What we call the introduction has more serious work to do than introducing—it creates a need to read on. It convinces us that there is a question or issue or situation or prior text worth examining. Absent that orientation, the essay is, in Elbow's terms, all scratch but no itch. Students avoid bringing in alternative positions or problems with their thesis for fear of weakening the argument, when in fact, this complication can create a tension (not to mention a credibility) that might engage the reader. David Bartholomae has called this "the tyranny of the thesis" (1983, 311).

Although he does not use the term *narrative*, Elbow seems to be describing a narrative or story structure, a form of plotting with tension, complication, resolution. Cognitive researchers over the past thirty years have firmly established that stories are "psychologically privileged" (Willingham 2004), uniquely capable of holding our attention and facilitating comprehension. Mark Turner, author of *The Literary Mind*, puts it this way: "Narrative imagining—story—is the fundamental instrument of thought. Rational capacities depend on it. It is our chief means of looking into the future, of predicting, of planning, of explaining" (1996, 4–5).

THREE STORIES ABOUT STORIES

Our reliance on stories is rooted in a human need to determine causality. Thinking in causal terms is innate—we are hardwired to do it. There is clear survival value in this predisposition to think in terms of cause and effect, and we do it automatically. As an example—one Saturday morning, as I was loading groceries into my car, I heard a series of quick pops. I automatically asked myself, *What caused this?* and *What should I do?* They did sound like firecrackers—isn't that what people always say about shootings? But why would someone be shooting off firecrackers in a parking lot? I guessed it could be gunshots—and I needed to get in my car and leave as fast as I could, which I did.

So my instinct was to create two cause-and-effect narratives: What caused this? And what action will lead to my own safety? Naturally I wanted to fill in the narrative later—and the pops *were* gunshots, fired into the air by a mentally disturbed man, about seventy-five yards from where I was loading groceries. Had I been ten minutes later in shopping, I would have been in a lockdown in the grocery store for two hours as the shooter was talked into giving up.

It is misleading even to consider this initial reaction a deliberation: it was more a biological reaction, a frisson of fear and a reflex. Cognitive scientists suggest that our ability to react this way is an evolutionary survival tool, one that we share with other animals, with the robin who spots a hawk, the dog hunkering down in a thunderstorm. But we can elaborate and explain this instinctual moment in a story. In fact, we are troubled when we can't make a story of it, when, for example, we don't know a motive for a crime.

This two-part narrative (What has happened? What do we do about it?) is the foundation for any proposal for change. The result may not look like a narrative, but it is narrative to the core. To take another local example: Our small New England town recently engaged in a vigorous debate about removing a nineteenth-century dam. It was no longer operative as a mill, and the state had judged it deficient; the water quality in the pond retained by the dam had deteriorated. And the pond was overrun by vegetation. But to remove the dam would also remove the iconic mill pond that was a virtual symbol of the town, a beautiful entry point from the south. (I live on Mill Pond Road.)

Arguments from history came from both sides: the dam marked the area where the town was settled and was a reminder of the industry in the early community. Others countered that the history of the river predated the founding of the town, and the free-flowing river was used by indigenous communities long before the settlement.

So whose history was most relevant?

There was a question of whether the dam was responsible for the poor water quality or if it was the runoff from the town that entered the pond. There were also scenarios for the future. Could dredging take care of the excessive vegetation? What would happen if the dam were rebuilt? What would it cost? What would happen if nothing were done and the dam gave way? What would happen to the land that would be created by the pond's disappearance? Invasive plants? Would Great Bay (a tidal estuary) be damaged if all the material held back from the dam ran into it? What about property values for those losing frontage on the impoundment? It all came down to present (What is the problem?); past (How did we get here?); and future (What do we do about it?). The guts of civic deliberation. Ultimately the town voted resoundingly to take out the dam.

Establishing a convincing story is also central to trial law. I have had jury duty only once, and for whatever reasons, defense lawyers used their free challenges to remove me from all but one of the juries I was picked for. But I did serve on one aggravated drunk-driving case. Even before the crime was announced, I guessed it was a drinking case—the defendant's face was so flushed. As a jury we had to choose between two stories, expertly presented by the defense lawyer and the prosecutor. The prosecutor presented evidence that the defendant was driving a van erratically. But when a police officer put on his flashing lights and pulled up behind him, he saw the driver changing seats with the passenger. By the time he came around to the window, the passenger was in the driver's seat—and in court she testified that she had been driving that evening. Still the officer administered a breathalyzer and the man was legally intoxicated.

The defense lawyer began by taking us to see the van in question—and her case depended on the physical features of the van. She reminded us of the small window at the back, the one the officer looked through to see the supposed switch. She asked: Could he really be so sure of what he had seen through that window at night? Wasn't there a reasonable doubt here? And she pointed out the high console between the two front seats. It would take some acrobatics for the two people to have switched seats so quickly—was that plausible?

Our jury deliberated about two hours. On the issue of seeing through the window there was agreement that with the flashing lights illuminating the van, seeing a switch would be no problem. But what about the difficulty of making the switch? A couple of jurors, who had driven similar vans, confirmed it would be no big problem—and one admitted that he and his wife would make the switch *while driving* when they didn't want to stop. We voted to convict, and the judge entered the jury room and shared the defendant's previous list of drunk-driving convictions, which went to pages—and he informed us that in this aggravated case, a conviction would mean a minimum of one year in prison. It was a heartbreaking moment to return to the courtroom and to observe the red-faced defendant whose freedom was being taken away. These stories had consequences.

Was this trial about argument? Yes, but argument about which story made the most sense. Both lawyers were masterful storytellers.

THE DANGER OF THE SINGLE STORY

We naturally think of our storytelling capacity as a gift—and it is. But it is also a trap—what the Nigerian novelist Chimamanda Ngozi Adichie has famously called "the danger of the single story" (2009). We create stories instantly, effortlessly, often drawing on existing cultural scripts or stereotypes—in fact, it is misleading to say we create them, as the story type is already available. We just pluck it from the ether; it's already prepared. In *Thinking, Fast and Slow* (2011), Daniel Kahneman notes that if someone gives us two random words, we instantly connect them in some microscenario. Let's try it:

> graduation—eggs

I quickly connect them this way: after a graduation ceremony there is some rowdiness that leads to an egg fight and a real mess. No great creativity here, just a cultural pattern of letting loose after a big ceremony. (When my editor read this example, she thought it too harsh—"I think about making a great egg dish before graduation.") It's an example of what Kahneman calls fast thinking. As humans, we naturally economize effort. Drawing on these cultural scripts is unavoidable and often useful. We usually don't need to go beyond that first story and do any real cognitive work—what he calls slow thinking.

But as Adichie notes, the single story often aligns with a stereotype or bias—and she gives as an example the way her parents in Nigeria referred to their houseboy, who came from a family in a rural village. He was "very poor," always referred to as "very poor," and she imagined his family having nothing and living off the yams and old clothing Adichie's family sent. But on one occasion she visited this houseboy's family and was surprised to see a beautiful basket that the houseboy's brother had woven. There was nothing in the stories she was told about the houseboy and his family that allowed her to imagine this skill.

Critical thinking, I feel, means creating that second, or third, or fourth story. It means not settling for the most convenient and conventional explanation (i.e., the first story). It means creating some tension between explanations, creating conflict, an itch to be scratched, a problem to be resolved, alternatives to be sorted out. It means that when the focus is exclusively on one thesis, we have a single story. It means that the minimum number of theses a writer needs to create is two, not one.[1] It means, at times, thinking dangerously and dwelling in possibilities that might be initially foreign and repugnant.

Let me give an example.

There are few more familiar characters in American literature than Atticus Finch, revered for his unflinching physical courage, moral eloquence in the trial summation, and belief in the potential for racial progress. His advice to Scout early in the book has become a part of Americana:

1. Gerald Graff and Cathy Birkenstein develop this point—the need for more than one thesis—in their hugely popular writing guide *They Say/I Say: The Moves That Matter in Academic Writing* (2021). The point a writer makes should be in response to some prior claim or position.

> You never really understand a person until you consider things from his point of view . . . until you climb inside of his skin and walk around in it. (Lee 1960, 33)

Let's call that version of Atticus the first story.

But Atticus' judgment in the last part of *To Kill a Mockingbird* raises questions about how well he follows his own advice after the attack on his children. For one thing, he fails to imagine the possibility that Bob Ewell, whom he has humiliated in the Robinson trial, might enact revenge on him or Scout and Jem. After the trial, Ewell even lunged at Atticus, spat on him, and threatened to kill him (248). He also tried to break into Judge Link's house. But Atticus reassures Jem and Scout that he will settle down when the weather changes. In allowing his children to walk home from the Halloween party unattended, he tragically fails to appreciate Ewell's state of mind. Atticus even admits it: "I can't conceive of a man who'd—" (308). It takes Sherriff Tate to explain that Ewell is too much of a coward to attack Atticus but brave enough to attack his children. He isn't "out of his mind," as Atticus claims; he is evil.

As Scout offers her fragmentary description of the attack, Atticus infers that Jem may have been responsible for Ewell's death, and the case would have to come before the court, where Jem would surely be seen as acting in self-defense. Then, in one of the most dramatic and touching scenes in the book, Tate and Atticus debate the right way forward. It is the only place in the book where Atticus is confronted and backs down on an issue of justice. Tate is way ahead of Atticus in thinking through the crime; he sees no reason to believe that Jem, a thirteen-year-old boy with a broken arm, could have held off Ewell, grabbed his knife, and stabbed him. It was the reclusive Boo Radley who had surely done it with a kitchen knife, and no purpose would be served in bringing either into court. Tate is acutely aware of the stature of the man he is confronting, but he holds firm. He will not put the boy—or Boo—through a legal procedure. He will rule that Ewell fell on his knife.

Atticus protests that not taking this to court will be hushing it up, that he doesn't "live that way" (313). He will lose the respect of his children if the matter is resolved this way, and suspicion will hover over

Jem. As a lawyer, he believes in a procedure for determining guilt, and what Tate is suggesting violates this belief. To use his own words, he fails at this moment to "climb inside the skin" of Jem or Boo and imagine what the court exposure would mean for either of them. Tate is right, and Scout recognizes that exposing Boo would be "sorta like shootin' a mockingbird" (317). So Atticus even misjudges Scout—who doesn't lose respect for him.

To my mind, this second story is appealing. Atticus is noble but flawed. As the saying goes, we are all entitled to the defects of our virtues. And Atticus has his blind spots. He becomes complacent about his children's safety because he cannot imagine Ewell's state of mind. He also thinks rigidly about what to do after the attack, failing to imagine the consequences of exposing Jem and Boo to legal action. In this case, Atticus' rectitude fails him.

KILLER DICHOTOMY

I began this chapter by challenging the way we have defined types of writing. I believe that students come to create an even more brutal division: creative and noncreative writing. It's a killer dichotomy. Obviously on the creative side are the poem, the fictional story, and perhaps the memoir. All narrative writing falls on the creative side. Noncreative writing includes exposition, argument, and the various kinds of analytic writing teachers ask them to do. This noncreative writing is sometimes loosely called academic writing. As an academic writer myself, I detest this binary; in fact, I detest the way *academic* is so often used as an adjective, like at the end of a lopsided game, when the scoring is "all academic now."

What most students envision as academic writing, I am convinced, is bad academic writing. It exists. And it is sometimes expected of students, but not as often as they think. In bad academic writing, the writer takes what Wayne Booth calls "the pedant's stance" (1963), assuming that the subject matter and the information they have uncovered are enough to compel the attention of the reader. The writer fails to ground the work in examples or stories, which could provide a respite and human anchor. Almost invariably there is an aversion to paragraphing, as if the detail is just too damn important to break it up into manageable units for the reader. In the parlance of reading specialists, these texts are inconsiderate.

But good academic writing—Laurel Ulrich's *A Midwife's Tale* (1991) or William Julius Wilson's *When Work Disappears* (1997)—makes good use of narrative tools. These writers illustrate wider social issues (the changing medical profession in the nineteenth century; the disappearance of factory jobs in urban areas) by introducing us to real people caught up in these changes. Even more formal academic papers need to create what I have called a narrative arc—there is some question or issue in their area of study that needs exploring. Maybe it is a neglected population causing a bias in research findings, or an unaddressed social problem, or a generally accepted truth that doesn't fit emerging evidence. There is some *trouble*. And the writer takes us on an inquiry to resolve the question, propose a path forward, or at least better understand the problem.

To those students put off by noncreative writing, I want to say: Academic writing is not what you think. You will meet teachers eager for you to build a personal connection to the topic, to put your own life story alongside the writing in the field. In writing about autism, your experience with an autistic brother is relevant. It is not merely anecdotal. You will meet teachers who don't want you to be locked into a formula, particularly where you settle for the easy thesis; they will want you to ask good questions that don't have easy answers. They will want the second and third stories. They will show you that academic work is personal—real, the creation of frequently eccentric and obsessed people, fascinated with their topics. Come on in.

MAKING AMENDS

When I was in graduate school, my advisor, James Kinneavy, modestly remarked, "My original ideas are those for which I've forgotten the source." This admission could fit on my own tombstone should I ever buy one. It would be fitting—one last, unacknowledged theft.

I remember one embarrassing moment when I met the legendary writing educator Peter Elbow for the first time; I picked him up in Boston and drove him to Durham for a talk. On the way he asked me about teaching writing at UNH, and I went on for miles about how my students were often blocked, overconcerned about audience to the point they couldn't get anything down, and they had to write freely, nonstop, just getting words on the page, outrunning the mental censor. Only as I was making the turn in Portsmouth did I realize that I had learned all of this from *Writing Without Teachers*, by Peter Elbow (1973), the man in the car.

When I began work on my own book *Minds Made for Stories* (2013), I felt pretty bold claiming that narrative was more than a type of writing—that it was better understood as the primary way we understand ourselves and our world. It seemed so radical that I wondered if anyone would take me seriously. As I read more about the topic, I had the opposite concern: that given the cognitive research of the past thirty years, and exhaustive testimonies of writers, it was so obvious, self-evident, that no one would pay attention.

After I finished the book, I continually ran across quotations I wished I had used, including one from my mentor and friend (and neighbor) Donald Murray. To make amends to him and all the others who entered this territory before me, I will give Don the last word:

> We study all the variations of narrative in short story, novel, stage, screen, and television drama, but rarely examine the narrative that is embedded in all effective writing—the proposal for a new marketing plan, the essay on health care, the insurance investigator's report, the sermon, the college scholarship application, the restraining order appeal, the memorial service remarks, even lab and book reports.
>
> If we are to become successful writers and rewriters, we must develop the craft to create and then hide the narrative that underlies most successful writing. The reader does not need to see the narrative any more than we need to see the intestines of the writer, but the narrative and the human organs both must be in place and working. (2004, 89–90)

Chapter Seven

MULTI (MULTIMODAL, MULTILITERACIES, MULTIGENRE)

Multi: The *multi* of this chapter celebrates the ways in which sometimes disparate modes, genres, and media are combined, woven, in the act of composing. Members of the influential New London Group have argued, "The multiplicity of communications channels and increasing cultural and linguistic diversity call for a much broader view of literacy than portrayed by traditional language-based approaches" (1996, 60). Composing—or "designing"—often means finding ways to combine different modes of representation (visual, verbal, gestural, musical) to create "hybrids" and to break out of "page-bound, official, standard forms of the national language" (61).

If you enter Harvard's fabled Widener Library and walk up the marble steps toward the reading room, you'll come by the entrance to the book-lined rooms of the Harry Elkins Widener Memorial. It was created by the Widener family to honor his life, cut short when he perished on the *Titanic*. Just past the entrance, there is a simple book display case, at first glance the kind you might find in any library. But in this one, you'll see a copy of Shakespeare's First Folio and a Gutenberg Bible, one of only twenty-three complete volumes in existence.

I would wander into this sanctuary whenever I could find an excuse to go into the Widener, and I was always stunned by the beauty of the Bible. The great achievement, of course, was Gutenberg's use of movable type, which would revolutionize printing, even spawn wars as the Bible became available in translations. But what surprised me was the elaborate designs and borders, a technique called rubrication. For example, the first letter of a passage was elaborately hand-illustrated; the borders sometimes featured vines and fruit or simply swirls and loops (see Figure 7.1). Maybe there is a lesson in this: that even as Gutenberg was creating possibilities for creating print, he could not neglect the readers' expectations for mixed media, for oversized ornate letters sprouting flowers.

It may seem a leap to move from this invaluable treasure of Western history to two boys' immersive experience in reading manga books featuring warfare. But the same point can be made: namely, the preference for print to work interactively with other modes of expression. Reading (and particularly writing) for children is often not a placid, solitary act of comprehension or composing. More often it is an *event*, rich in gesture, sound, image, and talk with friends, what Anne Dyson has called "social work" (1993, 7). Literacy researchers Kevin Leander and Gail Boldt brilliantly captured the dynamics of a reading event, as they followed ten-year-old Lee and his friend Hunter as they read two Japanese graphic novel (manga) series, InuYasha and Naruto. Here is how Lee's day began:

> Lee got up at 8:00 a.m., came into the living room of his home, settled into a chair and immediately began reading InuYasha. After about 30 minutes, he put the book down and went to his bedroom to retrieve a headband and several plastic toy daggers from his costume play collection of Naruto toys. Lee returned to his chair, put the headband on, arranged the daggers carefully around him, and went back to reading. As he read, he seemed unconscious of the fact that he often touched or adjusted his headband and touched, held, or rearranged the knives. Sometimes while

Epistola

Incipit epistola sancti iheronimi ad paulinum presbiterum de omnibus divine historie libris. Capitulum primum

Frater ambrosius tua michi munuscula perferens detulit simul et suavissimas litteras: que a principio amicicias fidem probate iam fidei et veteris amicicie preferebant. Vera enim illa necessitudo est et christi glutino copulata: quam non utilitas rei familiaris, non presentia tantum corporum, non subdola et palpans adulacio: sed dei timor et divinarum scripturarum studia conciliant. Legimus in veteribus historiis quosdam lustrasse provincias, novos adisse populos, maria transisse: ut eos quos ex libris noverant: coram quoque viderent. Sic pitagoras memphiticos vates, sic plato egiptum et architam tarentinum, eamque oram ytalie que quondam magna grecia dicebatur: laboriosissime peragravit: ut qui athenis magister erat et potens, cuiusque doctrinas achademie gignasia personabant, fieret peregrinus atque discipulus: malens aliena verecunde discere: quam sua impudenter ingerere. Denique cum litteras quasi toto orbe fugientes persequitur, captus a piratis et venundatus, tyranno crudelissimo paruit, ductus captivus vinctus et servus: tamen quia philosophus: maior emente se fuit. Ad titum livium lacteo eloquentie fonte manantem, de ultimis hispanie galliarumque finibus quosdam venisse nobiles legimus: et quos ad contemplationem sui roma non traxerat: unius hominis fama perduxit. Habuit illa etas inauditum omnibus seculis celebrandumque miraculum: ut urbem tantam ingressi: aliud extra urbem quererent. Apollonius sive ille magus ut vulgus loquitur, sive philosophus ut pitagorici tradunt, intravit persas, pertransivit caucasum, albanos, scithas, massagetas, opulentissima indie regna penetravit: et ad extremum latissimo phison amne transmisso pervenit ad bragmanas: ut hyarcam in throno sedentem aureo et de tantali fonte potantem, inter paucos discipulos de natura, de moribus ac de cursu dierum et siderum audiret docentem. Inde per elamitas, babilonios, chaldeos, medos, assirios, parthos, syros, phenices, arabes, palestinos, reversus ad alexandriam, perrexit ad ethiopiam: ut gignosophistas et famosissimam solis mensam videret in sabulo. Invenit ille vir ubique quod disceret: et semper proficiens, semper se melior fieret. Scripsit super hoc plenissime octo voluminibus phylostratus. capitulum ii.

Quid loquar de seculi hominibus: cum apostolus paulus vas electionis et magister gentium qui de consciencia tanti in se hospitis loquebatur dicens. An experimentum queritis eius qui in me loquitur christus. post damascum arabiamque lustratam: ascenderit ierosolimam ut videret petrum et manserit apud eum diebus quindecim. Hoc enim misterio ebdomadis et ogdoadis: futurus gentium predicator instruendus erat. Rursumque post annos quatuordecim assumpto barnaba et tyto, exposuit cum apostolis euangelium: ne forte in vacuum curreret aut cucurrisset. Habet nescio quid latentis energie vive vocis actus: et in aures discipuli de auctoris ore transfusa: fortius sonat. Unde et eschines cum rodi exularet et legeretur illa demosthenis

Figure 7.1 *Page from the Gutenberg Bible, 1455*

> reading or looking up from his reading, he would practice hand gestures or looks, or verbalize sound effects, words, or phrases that were in the text. Sometimes he leaped out of his chair to try a particular pose or move, and then sank back into the chair to continue reading. (2013, 26)

Later in the day Lee's friend Hunter came over and the boys gathered their weapons, headbands, costume accessories—and books—and went to the porch to read, surrounded by these artifacts. At times during the reading, they would, seemingly spontaneously, erupt into play fighting with the weapons for few minutes, then return to their books. Later in the afternoon they went on fan websites, drew complex scenes involving characters and weapons, and played with Naruto cards. When Lee's father, himself an InuYasha fan, came home from work, he and Lee got into a discussion of the difference between the TV version and the book version. And finally at 8:00, when Lee's mother returned home, she found husband and son sitting at the dining room table reading manga.

This may seem an extreme example, but any casual observation of children's play confirms the claim that they favor multimedia; they favor combinations (Horn and Giacobbe 2007). If they are playing with a truck, they are commenting on what the truck is doing. If they are playing with *two* trucks, they are most likely crashing them into each other and creating sound effects. If they are drawing trucks (or maybe dinosaurs, as every boy does at some time), they will be narrating a story. No media exists singly; they combine, and it seems natural that way. Almost every beginning writer or drawer I have observed starts with the caption, a one-word label for an often complex drawing. In Figure 7.2, a five-year-old has long arms, seeming to reach and hold a cat—with the single word *tush* (touch). Ann Dyson (1986) argues that children coordinate multiple symbol systems, orchestrating talk, drawing, gesture, sound effects—and writing, which is emerging for young children, pulled along by the stronger systems.

For some neurodivergent individuals, the visual system is primary, and they struggle with exclusively verbal or print-based learning. This was the case for Temple Grandin (2023), who had no language until age four and was later diagnosed as autistic. Her thinking was—and still is—primarily visual. As a young child, she would play with making parachutes:

> I would spend hours tinkering and experimenting to figure out how to make parachutes, fashioned from open scarves, open more quickly each time I tossed them in the air. This required careful observation to determine how small design changes affected performance. (2023)

Figure 7.2 ***Child's Drawing with the Caption "Touch"***

But in school she struggled with subjects, like algebra, that had no visual component. She eventually found a home as an agricultural engineer, where she used her perceptual abilities to imagine farm building from the point of view of the animals.

Given this natural and early delight in multimodality—and the primacy of visualization for many learners—it's reasonable to ask what happens to it, particularly in school. What are the reasons for a transformation to what the New London Group has called "mere literacy" (1996, 64) that is, literacy conceived as limited to print only?

Surely the shift to a print-exclusive concept is due in part to the economies of production. While rubrication persisted at least for another century (Luther's Bible has similar adornments), it was an expensive, individual process—and rubricators, like contemporary toll plaza workers, soon found themselves out of work.

Early mass-produced illustrations were usually woodcuts or engravings, which were more expensive to produce than straight text. Photographic methods of book illustration were introduced around 1840. The first book using this technique was British botanist Anna Atkins' 1843 *Photographs of British Algae*, yes algae. Photographic methods continue to this day, but again color plates added expense to a book and had to be used sparingly. For example, the beautiful 1920 Scribner's edition of *Robinson Crusoe*, illustrated by N. C. Wyeth, had thirteen color plates in 368 pages.

There is also a tacit ideology in school—a sense of progression—where there is a weaning away from the visual. As already noted, the paper that children write on has progressively less space for illustrations: writing is viewed exclusively as producing text. And instruction in art or drawing is partitioned off to the art "special." Similarly, there is a rite of passage, a sense of being grown-up, when the child moves from picture books to chapter books, less dependent on illustrations. Standardized reading tests, a consequential definition of reading, provide unillustrated passages; tests of writing don't allow illustrations. And until relatively recently, many have seen forms of publication that lean on illustration (manga, graphic novels, comics) as a lower caste of writing. All this began to shift when Art Spiegelman won the Pulitzer Prize in 1992, and graphic novels such as Alison Bechdel's *Fun Home* and Neil Gaiman's Sandman series have since won critical acclaim and national awards.

These limitations were blown apart by the affordances of digital tools and platforms. Suddenly, it seemed, barriers went down and anyone with a computer could begin to do things, photograph and film things, integrate things—create—in a way that only specialists could before. Before there were gatekeepers—editors, producers, and publishers—who allowed would-be writers and moviemakers *in* or, more likely, kept them out. The door was now unimaginably more open. There would be open platforms for students to post their fan fiction about Harry Potter (nearly a million on Fanfiction.net); they could post videos on YouTube or Instagram, often reaching a real audience bigger than their school or maybe state. Easy (sort of) editing platforms, like iMovie and PowerDirector, enable anyone with a smartphone to create digital stories that bring together script, video, and music.

Suddenly, it seemed, barriers went down and anyone with a computer could begin to do things, photograph and film things, integrate things—create—in a way that only specialists could before. Before there were gatekeepers—editors, producers, and publishers—who allowed would-be writers and moviemakers *in* or, more likely, kept them out.

A case in point. In a building boom in schools after World War II, the intercom became a regular feature. They had been around for some time, having been invented in 1884, but in these new schools created for the baby boom, they became standard. Anyone from that period, or considerably later, can remember morning announcements, usually by the principal, droning on about meetings and schedules and forms that had to be filled out.

Flash forward to the new middle school in my hometown of Durham, New Hampshire, where there is a broadcast studio. For morning announcements, students sit behind a desk, with a digitally created background, usually of the new school, and announce the news (which they write), and they even have the possibility of inserting video clips of school events. It is broadcast onto screens in every classroom.

VENTURES INTO MULTIMODAL COMPOSING (TECH-LITE)

I am what might generously be called a "late-adopter" of new technologies. I stayed with the overhead projector well into the PowerPoint era—and

I only switched after an embarrassing experience at a conference. It was at Yale in a law school lecture hall, training ground for future presidents and Supreme Court justices. As I always did, I had asked for an overhead projector to show my transparencies. But when I got there I found the familiar surface for placing them—but no arm to project them to a screen. So, mildly panicked, I asked about it. My host explained that the system converted my transparencies to digital slides and projected from behind the screen. In effect it *turned my presentation into a PowerPoint*. Some attendees, in their evaluations, commented (not very positively) on my use of transparencies. So I took it as a sign to reluctantly move past my overhead days.

Suffice it to say, I am not the person to lead the way to innovative uses of technology. There are now many excellent books by agile adopters of new technologies for creating multimodal texts. I would recommend Shawna Coppola's *Writing Redefined: Broadening Our Ideas of What It Means to Compose* (2020). Also the "Digital Composition" chapter in Penny Kittle and Kelly Gallagher's *4 Essential Studies* (2021). But in this section I will focus on several ways of embracing multimodality that require little tech savvy.

Read-Alouds

Many of the things we do in class are multimodal, without our even thinking of them in that way. For example, as I have already noted, when I am responding to a student's paper, I like to pick a section that is well written—and read it aloud *as literature*. I want the student to *hear* that excellence. I want to bring in what the New London Group calls an aural modality. We do the same thing when we have celebrations and readings at the end of a unit, or what Scott Storm, a high school teacher in Manhattan, calls novel slams, where students read aloud an excerpt from the novel they are writing. Too often texts (both written and read) go silent as students move away from the primary grades.

There are also certain passages, often used as prompts for writing, that I loved to read aloud. One is from Calvin Trillin's "The Best Restaurants in the World," where he describes one of his favorite eateries,

Arthur Bryant's in Kansas City:

> When I am away from Kansas City and depressed, I try to envision someone was walking up to the counterman at Bryant's and ordering a beef sandwich to go—for me. The counterman tosses a couple of pieces of bread on the counter, grabs a half pound of beef from a pile next to him, slaps it on the bread, brushes on some sauce in almost the same motion, and then wraps it all up in two thicknesses of butcher paper in a futile attempt to keep the customer's hand dry as he carries off his prize. (1984, 384)

I love that "for me." There is a running argument in the essay about best restaurants—unresolvable because of a universal bias for the restaurants from our neighborhood and hometown. And that is what I invite students to write about. My own choice is the Dairy Bar in Ashland, Ohio, where one can find the best milkshakes in the world.

Formats

There are also simple, no-frills ways of playing with the format of writing to enhance visual appeal. I'll confess that for years I assigned the generic persuasive paper and didn't think too much about format except to say it should be double-spaced and twelve-point type. Only way too late in my career did I decide that I should specify a real genre, the op-ed column, and that I should require three formatting features.

- A headshot—and it was so interesting to see how they presented themselves. I could barely recognize some of my students who wandered into my morning class in a sleepy daze, a few still in pajamas.
- A real title, something with an argumentative edge that might provoke interest. As my mentor Don Murray would drum in my head, there is a difference between a label and a title.
- A quote pulled from their piece, which they placed in a text box—this should be some well-crafted sentence that captured

> the key point of the column. It was a requirement that pushed them to identify the crux of their argument.

I can't reliably say that the writing was better, but it did seem to me that, with their photo facing the reader, they took more ownership of the writing.

The Songs of Our Lives

A friend of mine told me about her son's decision to be a philosophy major in college. This took her by surprise and she asked him why. "Well," he said, "I think it will help me with my songwriting."

At first this connection bewildered me, but as I thought about it, I realized songs are powerful forms of reflection, consolation, and memory. Particular songs seem to evoke times in our lives—my third-grade daughter dancing to Toni Basil's "Mickey." (We all loved the music video, Basil in her high school cheerleading outfit.)

Jeff Wilhelm built on this kind of connection at his National Writing Project site. Near the beginning of the project, participants chose a song that in some way was meaningful to them. They downloaded the lyrics for us, played the song, and wrote a reflection about why the song was significant—which they shared with the group after the playing. I happened to be attending during this time and was invited to pick a song. I chose Neil Diamond's "Sweet Caroline," which plays at the end of the seventh inning at all home Red Sox games—and everyone sings along, repeating at full volume, "So good, so good, so good." No matter the score.

I tried a variation of this as a short writing assignment early in a writing course. I similarly asked students to pick a song that reminded them of an important time in their lives and to download the lyrics (if they didn't already have them memorized—usually the case). Then I asked them to write about that time, what they did, where, who was with them, what the song said to them—interspersing the song lyrics in the remembrance. Some of them shared this writing and played the song that they chose.

Photography—Trusting the Twelfth Picture on the Roll

In the movie *Smoke*, cigar store manager Auggie Wren, played by Harvey Keitel, takes a photograph of the same New York City street scene each day at the same time. He has hundreds of these photographs, which he tries to show Paul Benjamin, a novelist who comes into the store. Reluctantly, Paul begins to look through the photographs and says that to him they all look the same—but Auggie corrects him:

> You've got your bright mornings and your dark mornings. You've got your summer light and your autumn light. You've got your weekdays and your weekends.
>
> You've got your people in overcoats and galoshes, and you've got your people in T-shirts and shorts. Sometimes the same people, sometimes different ones. (Auster 1995)

We have the cigar store owner giving the novelist a lesson in detail.

Bruce Ballenger, a gifted teacher in the University of New Hampshire writing program, built an assignment sequence on this same connection of photography to writing, what he called "the power of photography as a metaphor for the writing process" (2001, 29). The unexposed roll of film had an "uncanny resemblance to the blank page" (29). Obviously the term *roll of film* will be as unfamiliar to students as *correction tape* and *party phone lines*. But his assignment is even more accessible now as everyone has a camera and no one has to take a roll of film to the drugstore to be developed.

The first step was to take a series (roll) of photographs of anything they chose. Predictably, few students took more than one picture of any subject—and the photographs they took captured their subjects in the most obvious way. It was analogous to the first draft of writing, in which the student had not pushed beyond the obvious; they had made no discoveries. To do that, they needed another stage, another roll.

In the second stage they picked one of their original photographs and did a series on that one subject, varying angle, focus, light—to see the extraordinary in the ordinary. One of his students began with a conventional shot of an older campus building. But in the second round, he became fascinated with an iron fire escape on the wall of an older campus building.

> [The student] spent an hour taking pictures of the patterns of metal in the thick light of a late April evening. In some of the photographs, the fire escape seemed to cling to the building's brick like some outlandish bug, a black tangle of legs against the blue sky. These he shot while lying on his back. (32)

The final part of the assignment was to arrange the photographs in some theme and share them with the class. One student presented a series of images that captured students drinking—jumbled cans and half-empty whisky bottles:

> One particularly arresting image showed a student sitting in a chair with his head on the table nestled in a tangle of arms, asleep. Next to him was an empty bottle of Southern Comfort. The scene seemed deceptively peaceful if it weren't for the empty bottle. (38)

The process of visiting and revisiting their subjects—changing angles, distances, lighting—led to discoveries, a lesson to writers "to trust the process of looking and looking again, and looking closely to see what others miss" (40).

Spoken-Word Poetry

"Visceral, in your face, in your ears, in your snapping fingers, and tapping feet" (Black Youth Project 2011), spoken-word poetry has roots in the blues, the Harlem renaissance, and hip-hop music, as well as the interactive performances of the Beat poets in the 1960s. Poetry slams can be traced to the mid-1980s in Chicago. Marc Kelly Smith, a construction worker, felt that poetry had lost its passion and appeal. So he arranged for performances and contests, with poetry using the language of the people to be judged by the people. This poetry was accessible, emotional, personal, political, gestural, often alliterative and rhyming—sometimes second cousin to the rant. It broke the bounds of decorum.

Dennis Magliozzi, a high school teacher in my area, has brought this poetry into his courses, and he has created a club that holds slams and enters competitions. He introduced me to one of his students, Marley, who wrote a slam poem titled "Cauldron" in her ninth-grade English class with Dennis. Her poem conveys the intense anxiety, "a constant anguish snaking up your spine," she felt upon entering high school, after the difficult pandemic year in eighth grade. Her goal, she said, was for the reader to "feel what you are experiencing in the moment you are writing it." She uses the extended metaphor of being trapped in a witch's cauldron.

> The stew of
>
> Thoughts,
>
> Worries,
>
> And
>
> Fear
>
> Pour over my soul
>
> Drowning me
>
> In a potion
>
> Of my own creation.

The anxiety builds to a panic attack, which she represents in capital letters:

> I CAN'T BREATHE
>
> I CAN'T THINK
>
> I CAN'T

I CAN'T

Try.

I CAN'T

Still try.

She is rescued when a "calloused hand appears":

A sign of hope,

The sliver of light

At Midnight.

This hand brings her "back to/Reality" out of the "Hell-broth." She has

Another chance

To begin

Again.

There is some ambiguity in this ending. Begin what? A new start on a less anguished life? Or a process that will return to this same desperate feeling? She said maybe both—"It's definitely a spiral."

I asked her to read it for me, and her voice built to the desperation of "I CAN'T BREATHE." She gestured frantically and held her head as she said these lines. And her voice calmed as the calloused hand rescued her. I asked about it being calloused, and she said it was from so many rescues in this acidic cauldron. Voice and speech were significant in the composing process. "As I wrote it, I began to hear it more, and hear myself in it. I would listen to the poem in my head—I could hear my voice building up."

The calloused hand was, for Marley, a symbol of the advice and support and effort that could rescue her from the cauldron. I asked her if writing the poem was part of this help.

> *I think it did a little bit because I was able to let people know about this anxiety. It was normally out of school or I would try to hide it. That's another thing because conforming to the expectations of others, it's hard to fit in when you're going through something like this. You would try to hide it but there were subtle things that showed it like the constant tapping of the leg or fidgeting with my fingers. It helped me let the public know that I struggled with it and it helped me in that sense.*

The emotional openness of spoken poetry, even the expectation of strong emotion, seemed to open the door for her.

The Multigenre Research Paper

Although we can give names to certain kinds of writing (story, essay, argument) or to various modes (classification, definition, description), in reality good writing is a mix. Multi. And for good reason. We can talk about organization as a key trait of writing, but in our reading experience, motion is far more significant. As Peter Elbow reminds us, we experience reading in *time*, not as some timeless structure.

So what keeps us moving in time?

Clearly one trait is skillful alternation, moving from one mode or genre or mood to another. Action invites reflection. Argument needs story. A story needs a statistical context. An assertion needs an example. Long needs short. Seriousness needs lightness. This alternation sustains our attention and keeps us reading, moving. It's a kind of textual biodiversity, and writing is healthier for it. Writing is rarely one thing. And some works, like *Walden*, defy classification—part botany, part philosophy, part memoir, part social criticism, part poetry.

The multigenre research paper invites students to exploit this textual diversity. Most of the great ideas in literacy education emerge from the lore of practice, making it difficult to locate an originator. Was it Katie Ray or Carl Anderson who first used the term *mentor text*? Or did they get it from someone else, lost to history? But there is no doubt who invented the multigenre research paper: Tom Romano (2000). He came up with it when he was teaching high school in the late 1980s. Tom was always looking for ways to make academic work more appealing and artful; he himself is a masterful storyteller, and he infused this skill in his writing for teachers.

He came across Michael Ondaatje's *The Collected Works of Billy the Kid* (1970), a kind of history of the last two years of William H. Bonney's life. What attracted Romano's attention was the way Ondaatje combined a range of genres: poetry, reporting, narration, interior monologue—juxtaposing them without connective tissue. Yet behind this collage of forms was Ondaatje's own research into Bonney's life and the events of his death at the hands of the unrelenting sheriff Pat Garrett. Romano thought this was a form that could appeal to students and teachers. It would require the same researching skills as the traditional report, but writers could use that research, transformed, in a range of genres.

Laura LaVallee, an English teacher at Portsmouth (NH) High School, took a summer course from Tom as he was developing this idea—and she became a devoted multigenre enthusiast. I decided to reconnect with her to see where she has taken the idea. In our interview, she noted that students often associated writing with the school essay—a tightly controlled, sometimes formulaic type that gave them little agency (and little pleasure). They had to operate "in this box," making no decisions about form and often content. I had heard this from students I'd interviewed, like Alyssa, an eighth grader who lamented, "It's almost like an essay strips imagination from kids" (in Newkirk 2021, 26). Laura noted that her students even failed to count other kinds of composing—tweets, posts, emails—as writing at all.

Her MGP assignment gave students the opportunity to choose both topic and the various genres they might use to explore that topic. Initially she might give them a list of possible genres, some fairly obvious and traditional (poetry, short fiction, profile, business letter), others less expected (doctor's note, timeline, horoscope). But students often went beyond this list, bringing in unexpected genres. For example, a student in a culinary arts program explored her fascination with bread. Laura told me:

> *In her paper she describes this bread truck that she dreamed of owning when she was older. And one of the genres she tried involved five different bread recipes, so she researched the recipes—and actually made the bread. She had kids taste the bread and she made a graph from the results.*

Laura admitted it was a project she "wouldn't have thought of in a million years."

Another student, writing about five key scenes in *Catcher in the Rye*, dug up his old Lego kit and made constructions for each scene, which he then wrote about. When students see these out-of-the-box genres, it prompts more innovation.

As might be expected, the MGP is also multimodal, inviting students to bring in talents that they might think ill-suited for an English class. Laura said:

> *A lot of them have these talents that they're not able to show off. If they're an artist, they get to show off that craft in art class. If they're musically talented, it's only in music class where they can show what they can do. Here's an assignment where I'm saying, "Cool, paint a picture for me about this," or, "Write an original song that you can perform." So they're able to take these interesting talents they have outside of school and use them in an English class.*

These papers *do* require research, but not always the traditional kind. One student who wanted to explore her Italian ancestry did extensive family interviews and spent time on Ancestry.com. Another, writing about *The Office*, binge-watched fifty episodes to gather material. The food truck student researched recipes and did a survey. Still, Laura expects them to use the conventions of citation.

The MGP assignment culminates in a celebration, with students sharing parts of their papers. Laura told me a story about one such ending, early in her career. She had what she called an open mic reading, and all of her students shared, except one who passed. It was a young woman, from a troubled home, who had just "shut down" in the previous weeks.

After the reading, Laura went around the room with her shopping bag, collecting papers, and was about to skip over this student, but the girl reached back in her backpack and brought out her paper and put it in the shopping bag.

After the class, during lunch period, two students stayed in the class to thank her for assigning the paper ("How often does that happen?"). One had written on depression; she was, in Laura's words, "very vulnerable and brave." The other student wanted to say how much the paper had helped her, as she had been dealing with some of the same issues. "It was a really great moment." When they left, Laura pulled out the paper that she hadn't expected to get:

> *I can't remember the title, but I remember the first page—there was a sonogram picture. And the student had had an abortion the previous week. That explains so much, right? And to process this, and what she had been through, she wrote the MGP about what had happened to her. It was so fresh. It had a letter to her unborn son, the sonogram, an obituary. I'll never forget that moment because I realized that this was such a safe place. And if I'd assigned a personal narrative, I'm not sure if she would have felt comfortable telling that story—or telling that story in the traditional essay form.*

When writing about such emotional topics, the writing is often messy, confusing, and raw. "We can't expect students to write eloquently about trauma because there's nothing eloquent about it" (Newkirk 2021, 78).

Understandably, opening the door to these emotional, even traumatic, topics can make teachers uneasy. Few of us are trained as therapists—and it can seem that we are put in that position. It was an issue I dealt with as a director of a large university writing program, where students would often take up these tough topics. Clearly each situation is different, and there are legal reporting rules, and on occasion some teachers need to advise students that they can seek counseling. But in general students were *not* asking us to be therapists. They wanted us to be writing teachers. They had taken us up on our invitation to write on topics of urgent importance and expected us to help with that writing. Or at least to be respectful readers, witnesses.

Paradoxically, writing can be therapeutic without teachers acting as therapists (Pennebaker and Evans 2014). If we exclude topics like depression, anxiety, and trauma, we send the message that they are unwriteable, outside the bounds of appropriate expression in a writing course. This doesn't make them go away, only stay underground. It keeps the stigma in place. Unlike traditional counseling, there is a thirdness to writing: there is the teacher, the student, and this third thing, the writing. As teachers, we can do what we do best: find strengths, encourage expansion, nurture reflection—we can act on the writing. The act of writing, and rewriting, can give shape, story form, and public meaning to feelings that can feel inchoate and uniquely personal, even shameful. That is the therapeutic value of writing. It also often makes for memorable, invested writing—not someone picking a standard topic on which they have no real interest like the legalization of marijuana (a very small benefit of the new current laws on marijuana is that this topic may be retired).

Even before the pandemic, the mental health of adolescents was a serious concern. "More than 1 in 3 high school students reported having persistent feelings of sadness or hopelessness in 2019, a 40% increase from 2009" (Molano 2021). The pandemic only made things worse, particularly for girls, with a *Journal of the American Medical Association* analysis concluding that there is an "urgent need for intervention and recovery efforts aimed at improving child and adolescent well-being" (Racine et al. 2021). Given this critical condition—with emotional distress being such a central part of students' lives—it seems inarguable that there must be a place for naming and reflecting on that distress. Otherwise we create a school that, in the words of psychologist Lev Vygotsky, "has been locked away and walled in as if by a high fence from life itself" (in Moll 2014, 121).

As teachers, we can do what we do best: find strengths, encourage expansion, nurture reflection—we can act on the writing.

YES, BUT

In 2022, the National Council of Teachers of English assembled a distinguished panel of educators to produce a position statement on media education in the language arts (Hobbs et al. 2022). They cite a member of the New London Group, Gunther Kress, who claimed that multimodality represents the "normal state of state of human communication" (2010, 1)—and that reform is needed to move English and ELA *beyond* "traditional reading and writing" practices. New genres, involving mixed media, need to be introduced. The position statement also argues that "the time has come to decenter book reading and essay writing as the pinnacles of English language arts education" (Hobbs et al. 2022, 2).

This last recommendation—"to decenter book reading"—drew a rejoinder from literacy specialist Mike Schmoker (2022), who argued that real book reading is hardly the central experience of many high school students. In his experience, an "alarming proportion" arrive without having ever read an entire book. Many of the new digital forms like infographics and posts and memes and tweets cater to shorter attention spans and fail to develop more sustained and consecutive capabilities.

It's a problem the media critic Neil Postman dealt with in his classic *Teaching as a Conserving Activity* (1979), though his concern was television. Postman felt it was a mistake for schools to mimic, or take direction from, the media environment students swim in. It should stand for something else: "the electronic information environment, with television at its center, is fundamentally hostile to conceptual, linear modes of expression" (74). The sustained reading of print can develop capacities that the distractive media culture undermines. It can build the capacity for attention for following an extended argument, for following the development of a character, for immersion, for *being the book*.

Forty years later, Postman's argument is reprised in deeply anxious books like Maryanne Wolf's *Reader, Come Home* (2018), Nicholas Carr's *The Shallows* (2010), and Sherry Turkle's *Reclaiming Conversation* (2016). Wolf sees the new media environment as undermining "cognitive patience" (2018, 46). She and other cautionary critics see young people in particular as being captive (they often use the term *rewired*) to digital media, thus losing valuable cognitive capacities and social skills that older generations, that is, traditional readers, possessed. It follows that schools, with their traditional focus on sustained language, should act as a counterweight to the media culture that is reliant on images, skimming, distraction, and immediate gratification.

There is something significant, I think, in the fact that the arguments put forward by Wolf and others are almost identical to the one Postman made about television forty years earlier. And if we look at what we were watching in the 1970s—*Mash*, *The Flip Wilson Show*, and *Marcus Welby, M.D.*—it seems so benign. Or if we go back a decade earlier, huge audiences watched *Gunsmoke* and *The Andy Griffith Show*. I mean, really?

I suspect we could find his "decline" narrative in every generation, as newer media, music, art forms "erode" established norms and tastes. A generation before Postman, you'd find comic books as the great contributor to what was then called juvenile delinquency. I also suspect that the younger generation can spot these narratives a mile away—and dismiss them. You know, "In my day, we had to walk all the way to the television set to change channels."

The thrilling aspect of the New London formulation is the focus on *design*. Where before, students were spectators and media literacy focused on critique and analysis, now they can be makers; they can be players. Where before, to make a short film you needed a studio and an expensive camera, sound, lighting, and editing equipment, now you can use a phone with some easy downloads. There is no turning back from these affordances, just as there was no turning back from Gutenberg's movable type. But there is a lot of catching up that we teachers need to do, and we'll probably need our students' help. And we'll need some humility.

But, I will also argue that it doesn't mean we should decenter book reading—the next and last big idea.

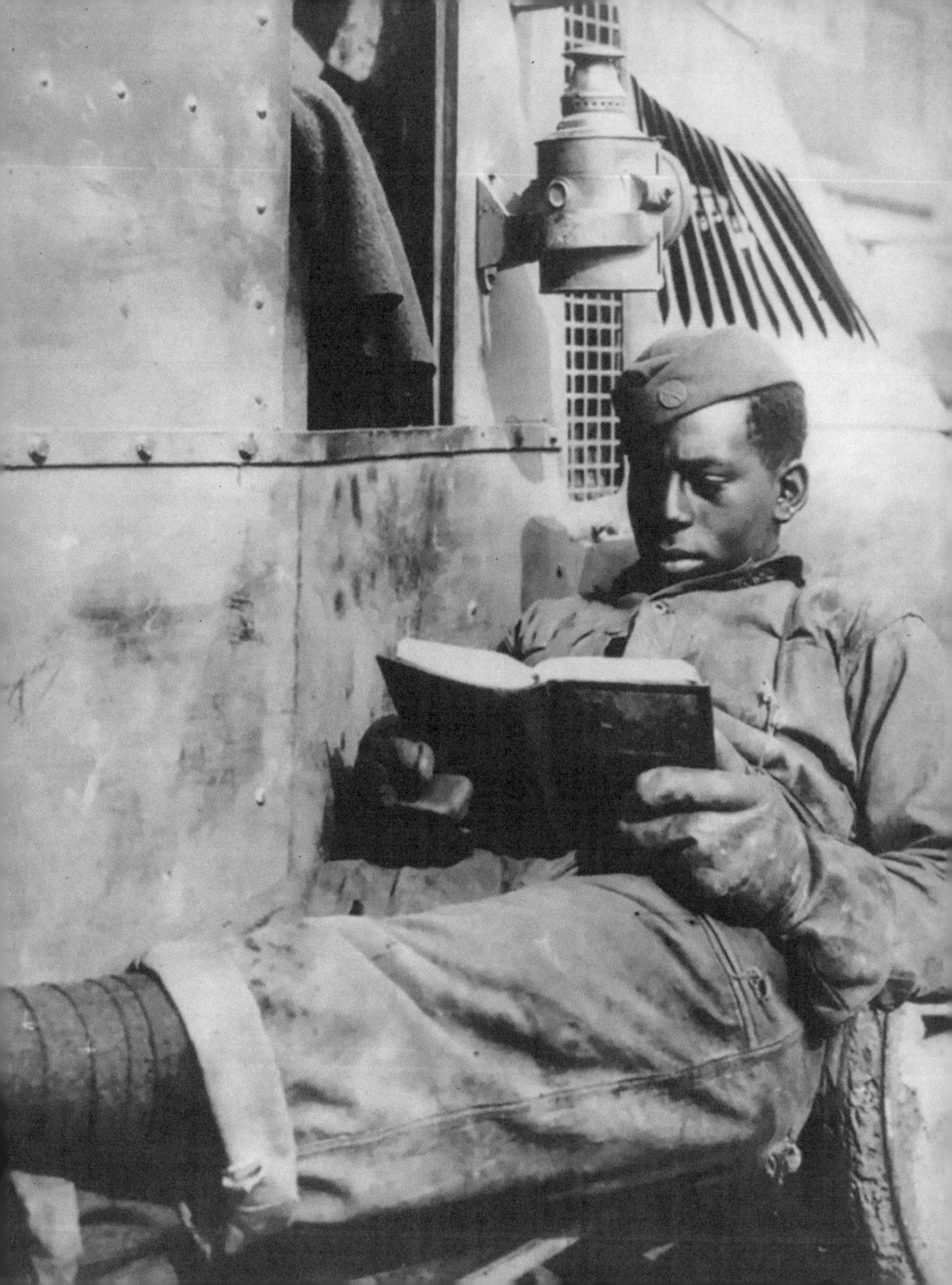

Chapter Eight

INDEPENDENT READING

Independent Reading: Independent reading is based on the seemingly obvious proposition that students will be more engaged, and become more proficient, if they have substantial choice in what they read. Research on the reading (or, more precisely, the nonreading) habits of students shows a significant decline around age nine (Scholastic 2019), and for most students, self-chosen, sustained reading is a microscopic part of their lives (Rideout, Foehr, and Roberts 2010). As a result, they fail to build fluency and stamina as readers—and they are overmatched by the books they are required to read, often developing fake reading as a coping strategy. A reading curriculum that denies choice and focuses primarily on teacher-chosen class novels usually fails to reverse this trend. An independent reading program, however, involves more than offering choice. It requires a rich set of supports: classroom libraries, time for in-class reading, book talks, modeling, and growth monitoring. As Nancie Atwell, a leading proponent, said to me, "It's not one thing; it's twenty things."

Each spring in our town, there is a period when residents can put just about anything on the curb—old sofas, desks, gerbil cages—and the town will pick it up. It's quite an event. Before the pickup time, people in flatbed trucks and vans cruise the neighborhoods, checking out the discards and loading up useful items. For years, there were numerous stationary bicycles out for pickup, and I was surprised that so many had been purchased.

Then it occurred to me. The *same* stationary bikes came out each year, only from different owners; they sort of circulated through the town. People would pick them up, maybe use them for a few weeks, then put them away in the basement until the next pickup. We even had one in our house. Though we all knew—logically—that keeping up this form of exercise was good for us, I suspect we found it repetitious and boring to keep at it. As psychologist Daniel Willingham (2017) notes, logical appeals rarely are enough to cause us to change behavior—we are more likely to be influenced by emotion and the pleasure we take in an activity itself.

To put it more formally, we do better at engaging in—and persisting in—activities that are *autotelic*: having a purpose in and not apart from themselves. We swim not because it will make us healthier (or less likely to drown); we swim because we love the sensation of our bodies afloat, moving through the water, as if it is our natural element. We read not for some future benefit, but because we love the sense of being in what Nancie Atwell and Ann Merkel (2009) called "the reading zone." This is not to say there aren't future benefits—extensive reading is probably the best predictor of academic success (Cullinan 2000), but that is more a by-product. The attraction of reading is in the moment of the doing; the purpose is within the act—it is not a means to something else. We would read even if there weren't that future benefit.

The corollary is that students who never have this sensation of "being the book" (Wilhelm 1996), of losing a sense of time and place as they follow characters and a plot, will find reading a task, completed under duress but avoided when possible. In fact, I would argue that unless you have entered this state, the whole point, the whole gratification of extended reading, is baffling.

What, after all, does a reader reveal? Virtually nothing. The reader is a picture of immobility. She is motionless. Not even the occasional twitches and taps that most humans need to maintain attention when they are sitting for long periods of time. Only the turning of pages every couple of minutes. The reader's face is impassive—there are no noticeable signs of response, no laughter, rare even a slight smile.

And what is it that so stills this reader? Printed words, thousands of them, maybe forty or fifty lines per page. No pictures, no sounds, no color. Endless combinations of twenty-six letters. And in this almost complete absence of stimulation, the reader can remain for an hour or more—and when finished, she feels momentarily disoriented as she transitions from one world to another.

Only by admitting to this oddness, this mystery, this affinity to mystical states, can we begin to account for the divide that separates reader from nonreader. The habit of extended reading, particularly novel reading, comes from the desire to enter and reenter a state of attention, and from the pleasure we gain in encounters with characters and storytellers, who become as real, sometimes more real, than actual people we know. But for reluctant or struggling readers, this zone is more a minefield, filled with long, unfamiliar words. The teaching question, then, is how to help readers enter this state of attention. And often the traditions of teaching novels get in the way.

CANONS TO THE RIGHT OF ME[1]

Going back to my days as a student in the 1950s and 1960s, novels appeared, often abridged, in the literature anthologies: double columns, lots of questions and footnotes to define unfamiliar words. That's how *Silas Marner*, disliked by students, and I think even teachers, was presented. For me it created a powerful dislike for George Eliot, erased only decades later when I read *Middlemarch*.

Why *Silas Marner* of all books? Well, it appeared on a uniform list of texts created by universities in the late nineteenth century, as did *Julius Caesar*, which was one of the earliest and most enduring selections—partly because Latin classes plodded through Caesar's *Gallic Wars*. The lists that

1. Ironically, this heading disfigures a quote from a poem of the old canon—"The Charge of the Light Brigade," by Alfred, Lord Tennyson. But I really remember it from the histrionic recitation by Alfalfa on the old TV show *The Little Rascals*—an illustration of how highbrow culture circulates and is mocked.

were created were, with the exception of Eliot, all male, obviously all white, and almost all British—Shakespeare, Milton, Burke, Scott, and Macaulay were among the most common selections. The US authors that made the lists—Irving, Whittier, Bryant—were clearly writing in styles modeled after British writers. There was no hint that the American renaissance of the mid-nineteenth century had even occurred (Applebee 1974).

Books that regularly appeared on these lists are often called part of a canon, a term that originally referred to ecclesiastical law but in the eighteenth century began to refer to books thought to have enduring, even sacred value. Matthew Arnold argued that this form of shared reading would take over the function of religion to help unify culture (we get echoes of this argument in E. D. Hirsch's promotion of cultural literacy). Almost immediately, social reformers like Jane Addams criticized these lists as elitist, promoting an Anglo-Saxon view of culture far removed from the lives of the immigrant children she worked with in Chicago (1908). The National Council of Teachers of English, founded in 1912, also opposed the domination of this college list.

While university-created lists no longer have authority over schools, there is an unofficial canon that has remained quite consistent: a 2012 survey revealed the most frequently taught books were *The Great Gatsby*, *Romeo and Juliet*, *The Crucible* and *The Odyssey* (tied), *To Kill a Mockingbird*, and *Night* (Stallworth and Gibbons 2012). The survey revealed that the list had slowly begun to diversify with the frequent mention of *Their Eyes Were Watching God*, *The Joy Luck Club*, and *The House on Mango Street*.

Books by Black authors (notably *The Color Purple*, *Beloved*, and *The Bluest Eye*) have often faced censorship problems, as does Sherman Alexie's *The Absolutely True Diary of a Part-Time Indian*—which was the number one banned book for the decade 2010–19 (American Library Association 2020). Alison Bechdel's graphic novel *Fun Home* has become a target because of its lesbian themes. And Maia Kobabe's *Gender Queer, A Memoir* was the most censored book in 2021. Organized nonprofits like Moms for Liberty have led opposition against LGBTQIA+ titles and have successfully supported legislation restricting their use in schools. In my own state Moms for Liberty established a five-hundred-dollar bounty for anyone successfully initiating action against a teacher for using questionable texts.

Educators of color have challenged this unofficial canon and argued for a more inclusive and restorative curriculum. The #DisruptTexts movement, originated and supported by Tricia Ebarvia, Lorena Germán, Kim Parker, and Julia Torres, has made skillful use of social media and traditional educational outlets to ask, Really? Why these books? Why not books by BIPOC (Black, Indigenous, and People of Color) authors? When we must use canonical texts, can we pair them with contemporary novels on similar themes by BIPOC authors? And how can we teach ourselves and our students to bring a critical lens to *all* the reading we do—posing questions such as "*Who is centered? Who is marginalized? Who is missing? And what does this mean and why does this matter?*" (2020, 101).

Take as an example Albert Camus' *The Stranger*, generally considered one of the greatest French novels. The central event of the book occurs when the protagonist, Meursault, kills an "Arab" whom he believes is threatening him on an Algerian beach. This "Arab" not only lacks a name in the novel but also lacks a personality, a history—he is simply a menacing "other." Camus' novel inspired the Algerian novelist Kamel Daoud to retell the story in his acclaimed *The Meursault Investigation*, giving "the Arab" a name, Musa, and telling the story from the point of view of his brother Harun. In an interview, Daoud commented ironically on this naming: "Ever since the Middle Ages, the white man has the habit of naming Africa and Asia's mountains and insects, all the while denying the names of the human beings they encounter" (2015).

The great African American educator Alfred Tatum has worked extensively with African American males in the Chicago schools, helping them build what he calls textual lineages. Books that become part of this lineage are those that help shape identity, that remain vital and memorable long after we read them, and that lead to other reading—building a genealogy. The stakes, as Tatum sees them, are high:

> Ultimately, each generation of African American adolescent males will judge for themselves whether to engage or disengage. Because these young men are unique and face their

> own challenges, they must identify texts that mark *their* times and *their* lives. If we create opportunities for this to happen in schools and other social institutions, they will not only begin to trust the texts, they will begin to trust us too. (2009, 139)

By contrast, he criticizes what he calls "disabling" texts that fail to do this, either because they are irrelevant to the lives of young men, or they caricature them, or they peg them at an embarrassingly low level of reading—he gives the example of a Berenstain Bears book used with a high school student.

Whole-class novels, chosen by the teacher or set in the curriculum, are often unwieldy to teach in heterogeneous classes, where there is a range of reading abilities. One obvious problem is that the traditional canon is slow to change, and books that speak to "*their* times and *their* lives" aren't on it, often deemed too controversial. But another issue is pace.

If one option readers crave is to choose their own books, another is to choose the pace and rhythm at which they read. Unlike other media, like movies, the reader controls time—we can decide to pause, can determine the proper pace for the book and for our own psycholinguistic processing. We can monitor our attention, reread if necessary, and determine the number of pages per reading session. In Italian this is called finding the *tempo giusto*, the right pace.

As a slow reader myself, I know how disruptive and unpleasant it is to be forced to read faster than my natural processing speed. Almost inevitably, in a whole-class situation, the established pace is too fast for some readers (who probably start finding shortcuts) and too slow for others, who read ahead and can muck up discussions. If we recall Charlie Chaplin's factory worker in *Modern Times*, his work is miserable because he has no choice in what he does, but at least as significantly, he has no choice in how fast he does it.

In these whole-class situations, students often figure out how to evade reading assigned books and still manage to get good grades—a process sometimes called fake reading. High school teacher Penny Kittle created a widely watched video (2010) in which she asked students about how they managed to pass tests and write papers on books they hadn't actually read. It was usually a combination of reading Sparknotes and listening to class discussions, where they picked up on key themes (like the American dream or man's inhumanity to man) and could find enough quotes. However, my favorite response came from a student who said he "talked to a kid who read Sparknotes"—even reading Sparknotes was too much of a commitment.

Finally, a word of caution. The Common Core State Standards for ELA are built on an assumption that students *are not reading hard enough material*. There is almost a fetish of difficulty. For example, they recommend that *Grapes of Wrath* (464 pages) should be a book for ninth and tenth graders, rather than the select older students who might read it now (NGA Center for Best Practices and CCSSO 2010, 58). (In fact, their Lexile scoring of the book has it at later elementary or middle school!) Let's be clear, this would be a guaranteed disaster, unfair to students—and Steinbeck. There will be a rush to Sparknotes, enriching the parent company (which I regret to inform you is Barnes and Noble).

THE PARADOX OF RESEARCH ON INDEPENDENT READING—A SHORT DIGRESSION

Once a man was on his knees, under a streetlamp, obviously looking for something. A policeman came by and asked him what he was doing.

"I'm looking for my keys."

"So is this where you think you lost them," the policeman asked.

"No," he replied. "But the light is better here."

I see this story as a kind of parable that explains why independent reading was not viewed as a validated practice in the influential *Report of the National Reading Panel* (National Reading Panel 2000). The National Reading Panel decided early on that it would focus on studies that could determine *causality*—which meant that it would limit its review to what is often referred to as the gold standard method: comparing experimental and control groups, so that one can determine the "causal variable."

Consider this method to be the streetlamp—it can shed light in some areas but not others. It usually works better on more easily quantifiable items (like word identification) than on more complex ones like comprehension, and it can barely touch some of the personal outcomes of reading that Tatum sees as central. Or if we view "engaged reading as a site for the development of a dialogic, relational self—the development of a human being" (Ivey and Johnston 2013, 254), standard, quantifiable tests (e.g., surveys and questionnaires) are not likely to shed much light.

Joanne Yatvin, the only classroom teacher on the eleven-person panel (think about that!), made this point: "From the beginning, the Panel chose to conceptualize and review the field narrowly, in accordance with the philosophical and research interests of the majority of the members" (2000, 444). And she rightly predicted that topics and methods that the panel did not examine would be seen as unsupported by research, even "failed practices" (446). The study does acknowledge that there is correlational data, actually lots of it (Cullinan 2000), that shows good readers read extensively—but what is the cause and what is the effect? Do good readers read a lot because they are proficient? Or do they become proficient by reading a lot? Or both—do the causal arrows go both ways, as Willingham (2017, 139) claims?

In order to explore the effects of an extensive, self-chosen reader, it is necessary to pick other research strategies, to shift the lighting to include student perspectives. In a profoundly important study, Gay Ivey and Peter Johnston (2013) interviewed seventy-one eighth graders who had spent a year in classrooms where teachers gave them choice in what to read, in the pace of the reading, and in how to respond to what they read. Teachers also gave them substantial time to read and supported them in book choice—each of the four classrooms had libraries of 150–200 titles, primarily young adult fiction. Ivey and Johnston coded the interviews for "causal statements" where students reported on the effects this approach had for them.

For some, it was the first time in their entire school career that they had "been the book" (Wilhelm 1996). One student put it this way:

> *Before the Fall* [by Lauren Oliver] is one of those, like, the first books I've ever truly gotten into, like one of those books where you could really picture yourself in that scene. Like you could feel you're with them. . . . I used to hate to read. I didn't read at all. I'd just sit there and turn the pages when the teacher looked at me, and that was pretty much it. (Ivey and Johnston 2013, 261)

Among the most often coded effects were

- engaged reading, being in the book
- conversations with peers about reading
- agency in what and how they read but also in shaping how they chose to act and the self they wanted to become
- stronger personal connections with peers
- knowledge of the world—and of other books (there were 317 mentions of specific titles)
- shifts in identity—in their sense of self

Although not a primary concern of the researchers, standardized reading scores also improved. According to students, the most important causal factors in this approach were choice, teacher behavior (book talks and recommendations), and access to books they found edgy and personally meaningful. In all, the study provides a powerful case for shifting away from class-assigned novels and from short (e.g., twenty-minute) reading times unconnected to the rest of the curriculum—toward a full, elaborated pedagogy of choice.

NOT ONE THING BUT TWENTY THINGS

I can proudly claim to be a footnote in the development of the reading workshop, in which chosen reading is central (Atwell 2015, 17–18). Around 1982, Nancie Atwell, then an eighth-grade ELA teacher in Boothbay, Maine, immediately adopted the writing approach, originated by Donald Graves, and invited me to visit. In her account, she claims that I admired the way she had taken on this approach, but I referred to it, undiplomatically, as "the writing ghetto." I explained that the way she taught writing, with conferences, individual goals, and choice of writing topics, seemed very separate from the more traditional, teacher-directed way she taught reading.

She credits this offhand comment as a prompt to shift her approach. I suspect this nudge was a microscopic factor; there was at the time an almost collective sense that it was simply incoherent to teach reading and writing so differently (Hansen 1987, Jensen 1984). Nancie soon altered her approach to make it more consistent—giving readers the same options as writers. And she documented this change in one of the most influential books ever written on literacy teaching, *In the Middle* (1987), and in the two editions that followed.

Independent reading, as she viewed it, was simple, at least in principle—supporting the activities of readers as they exist in real reading communities. But it was complex in enactment—not something that could be dropped into a traditional reading or literature approach, and not simply the unsupported offer to read whatever you want. As she said to me, "it's not one thing; it's twenty things."

There are many fine books that worked out this pedagogy of choice, including Penny Kittle's *Book Love* (2012) and her collaboration with Kelly Gallagher, *180 Days* (2018); Debbie Miller and Barbara Moss' *No More Independent Reading Without Support* (2013); Jeffrey Wilhelm and Michael Smith's *Reading Unbound* (2014); and, most recently, Ellin Keene's *The Literacy Studio: Reimagining the Workshop for Readers and Writers* (2022). It has been a labor of almost forty years. In the dwindling space I have, I will suggest only some of what those twenty things are.

Teacher Book Knowledge

If the goal is to put the right book in the right kid's hands at the right time, teachers need to have a prodigious knowledge of book possibilities. Even in the area of, say, sports literature, there are so many possibilities (Rodesiler 2022). Unfortunately, prospective ELA teachers are restricted in building that knowledge because they usually take (at most) one course in their entire preparation in children's or young adult literature—*one course* in the thirty-five or forty they take as an undergraduate. Not enough.

A Curated Classroom Library

Obviously. Teachers need an extensive library that includes a wide range of individual titles (including the classics)—nonfiction, realistic fiction, fantasy, horror, book series, graphic novels, authors of color, and group sets (four to five) for use in book clubs. The American Library Association recommends a ratio of twenty books per student with new titles introduced each year. There should be a range of difficulties and lengths, but no assigned reading levels. As Daniel Willingham writes, "books should not just be available, but virtually falling into children's laps, or at least visible in as many locations as possible: in the classroom, in every room of the house, in the car, and so on" (2017, 151).

Book Talks

Teachers and later students often take the floor to introduce books to the class. A book talk should be short (about two minutes), the speaker should have the book they're talking about in hand, and they should focus on the basic situation or conflict of the book. Penny Kittle noted that she sometimes would read a short excerpt to convey the style of the book. Atwell would have students rate the book on a scale of 1–10 and would feature top-rated books in a display area.

Volume

If reading (or maybe nonreading) is limited to a few class-assigned novels, young readers will not build the stamina and fluency they need; they're like runners who don't do their road work. Reading will be too discontinuous. One undeniable characteristic of a reader is always having a book going, feeling adrift if that isn't happening. One way to promote reading volume is the narcotic of counting: pages, number of books, a visible sign of growing competence.

Openness

There has always been a strand of elitism in American education that disapproves of subliterature, like comic books in the 1950s and dime novels in the late nineteenth century. For many teachers, vampire novels, gothic horror, and high fantasy are not part of their reading diet, and they may dismiss such books as incapable of eliciting thoughtful reading—unlike realistic, character-driven fiction, usually the foundation of adult reading groups. In *Reading Unbound*, Jeffrey Wilhelm and Michael Smith (2014) show that these disfavored genres can elicit thoughtful interpretations—the genres don't set a low ceiling on thinking or engagement.

We signal the importance of an activity by assigning time to it. If self-chosen reading is important, we must provide regular opportunities to read in class.

Time to Read

We signal the importance of an activity by assigning time to it. If self-chosen reading is important, we must provide regular opportunities to read in class. Continuity and momentum are so important for readers; often an interruption of a day or two causes us all to lose track of the book. Ivey and Johnston (2013) recommend that this time not be totally silent, so there can be some informal talk among students. They call it "somewhat silent reading." It is common to have a special reading time each day, with the expectation that this reading extends outside of class—with a page goal (twenty pages in Atwell's case) or a time goal, perhaps an hour in high school or less for younger children.

Reading Conferences

During in-class reading time, teachers can systematically touch base with students, asking versions of Carl Anderson's famous question, "How's it going?" (2000). Early in the year, students may choose books that are just too hard for them, and teachers can encourage them to make another choice—readers have the right to abandon books. In conferences, students share their thoughts, questions, and observations about the book, make predictions about what will happen, and even decide how to persevere in a challenging book.

Future Plans

One key expectation is planning for future reading—in Nancie Atwell's reading workshop, students keep a "Someday" list, which includes possible titles for future reading. Very simply, if a book talk seems appealing, students write the title on a notebook page. This sense of a reading future, of books on the horizon, is absolutely central to assuming the *identity of a reader*—it's a version of Tatum's lineages, the story of how reading choices lead to other reading choices, of how the reading culture of the class opens up appealing options. The anticipation of future reading builds momentum, creates direction.

Constructed Criteria

When I asked Ethan, a ninth grader, about what makes a good horror story, he shared this principle:

> Take something normal and make it wrong. Like something like a fight between a nephew and an uncle [the inciting conflict in his story]. Take that—that's not wrong—that's going to happen. That's life. Take something like that and make it go wrong. . . . Not some alien spaceship coming in from nowhere and blowing things up. It might be scary if you wrote it right but it's not going to be as scary as something like a dog going rabid in *Cujo* (King 1981). All of a sudden, you're looking at dogs and you're looking at them differently. (Newkirk 2021, 98)

No one handed this rule down to Ethan; he *constructed* it from his own reading of Stephen King, his mentor. Nancie Atwell told me she invites her students to construct criteria for whatever genre they read (and write). What makes a good book review? A good mystery? Even though she could bring in great lists from previous classes, she doesn't. It needs to start anew each year.

A Language to Talk About Reading

There are dictionaries of literary terms, and overfocusing on them can become an interference. Yet terms can be useful, even homegrown ones. For example, eighth-grade teacher Laura Bradley uses a variety of mentor texts to teach the concept of *inciting incident*, an event that occurs early in a novel that sets it in motion—Harry Potter discovering he has magical powers or Melinda Sordino being bullied in her freshman year in *Speak*. Other terms might be *dialogue*, *motivation* (of the characters), *point of view, setting*, *protagonist*, *the hero's journey*, *conflict*, and the various genres and subgenres that students might read. One of my favorite terms is *trouble*. As Janet Burroughs famously claimed, fiction is all about characters in trouble.

Minimal Interferences

If the goal of independent reading is to help students enter the reading zone, we need to avoid, or at least minimize, practices that get in the way, that interrupt, that take agency away from the reader. The number one culprit, in my view, is a list of comprehension questions at the end of a selection. One ninth grader I interviewed put it this way: "When I read I want to get lost in the world the author created, and when I have to answer questions it makes me feel I can't get lost anymore" (Newkirk 2021, 23). He has to be accountable to someone else's agenda, some authority's view of what is significant.

As much as possible, the focus should be on student-generated questions: what they wonder about, what puzzles them, how they judge characters (their flaws, their motivations, their relationships), what they predict will happen in the plot. Questioning has been solidly shown to be a powerful comprehension strategy (National Reading Panel, 2000) and it gives agency to the student.

Modeling Reading

As I've already noted, I regularly ask prospective English teachers if they have ever seen any of their professors demonstrate how they read a text *for the first time*. The answer is invariably no. Consequently, students might assume that their teachers never experience anything like the confusion they do—that, in fact, this confusion or difficulty is a failing on their part.

While there are any number of skills and practices a teacher can model, I would argue the most important is demonstrating the role of not knowing in the reading process. John Keats called this attitude a "negative capability": a willingness to embrace "uncertainties, mysteries, doubts, without any irritable reaching after fact and reason" (1899, 277). When reading fiction, we are often off-balance, puzzled, unsure of how to respond, confused, particularly early in a novel. And we need to dwell in that state for a while and not be "irritable." We need to model this puzzlement with sentence stems like "I'm not sure how I feel about . . . ," "I'm wondering why . . . ," and "I'm struggling in this part to . . ."

If we take Toni Morrison's *Beloved* as an example, I don't see how anyone reading the opening for the first time could say, "Sure. OK. I get it." I struggled just to get some foothold, some fragmentary sense of what was happening (and to be honest, I didn't finish the novel until my third try). I can think of few reading skills—or life skills—more crucial than the capacity to be in this unknowing state and to remain calm, trusting that with effort and attention we can move to greater clarity.

A Policy on Parent Complaints

As I write, there is a resurgence of book banning, famously including Art Spiegelman's Pulitzer Prize–winning graphic novel *Maus*. One concern was the nudity in the book (yes, but these are mice!). School districts should have procedures, including standing review committees with clear criteria, to handle complaints that would make a book unavailable to students. Without a policy, teachers are vulnerable to quick, and often embarrassing, decisions by panicked administrators in response to parental pressure.

Clearly the classics have a place in independent reading, in the curated library, in book talks. Often we can introduce students to an author with an excerpt, to plant a seed for future reading. I once saw a gifted British teacher hold a difficult fourth-form (tenth-grade) class spellbound by reading a passage from *A Portrait of the Artist as a Young Man* where Stephen is caned for accidentally breaking his glasses. I still retain the image of his throbbing hand seeming to crumple like a burned leaf.

The farm boys and girls who read *McGuffey's Fifth Eclectic Reader* (McGuffey 1879) got their first taste of Dickens with a short passage from *Nicholas Nickleby* describing Wackford Squeers' method of teaching.

> "We go on the practical mode of teaching, Nickleby; the regular education. C-l-e-a-n, clean, verb active, to make bright, to scour. W-i-n, win, d-e-r, der, winder, a casement. When the boy knows this out of a book, he does it." (250)

The push to force full-length classics on reluctant students is, in reality, an admission of defeat—it is built on the assumption that unless students are forced to read the classics, the books will never be read. Advocates of independent reading see the issue more as timing—readers will come to these works when they have built capacity and confidence through extensive reading of contemporary literature. Austen and Dickens, Morrison and Ellison will be there waiting and able to do their work.

FREE READING

In October 1941, my dad, Maurice Newkirk, a twenty-six-year-old teacher in a Tiffin, Ohio, orphanage where he himself was raised, published the first article of his career—titled "A Venture into Free Reading." It described an experiment in which he located all the novels he could get his hands on and brought them into a study hall, trying to match books with students—and he meticulously recorded their reading choices over the course of a year (each read about seven books during the year). Students avoided the established classics: Dickens, Tolstoy, and, hardly surprisingly, Joyce's *Ulysses*, which had just been cleared for distribution in the United States. But Jack London was popular, as was John Steinbeck's *Of Mice and Men*, which had just come out. It was an early version of independent reading, elaborated so carefully by Linda Rief, Nancie Atwell, and later Penny Kittle and Kelly Gallagher.

The date of the article is ominous: two months later, Pearl Harbor was bombed. He was soon inducted into the army, serving in New Guinea and the Philippines. Throughout the war my mother would send him Modern Library classics, which he read in the jungles where he was stationed. These books made their way back to our home, each with an inscription in his distinctive handwriting (we suspect he was a natural left-hander converted to right-handedness). (See Figure 8.1.)

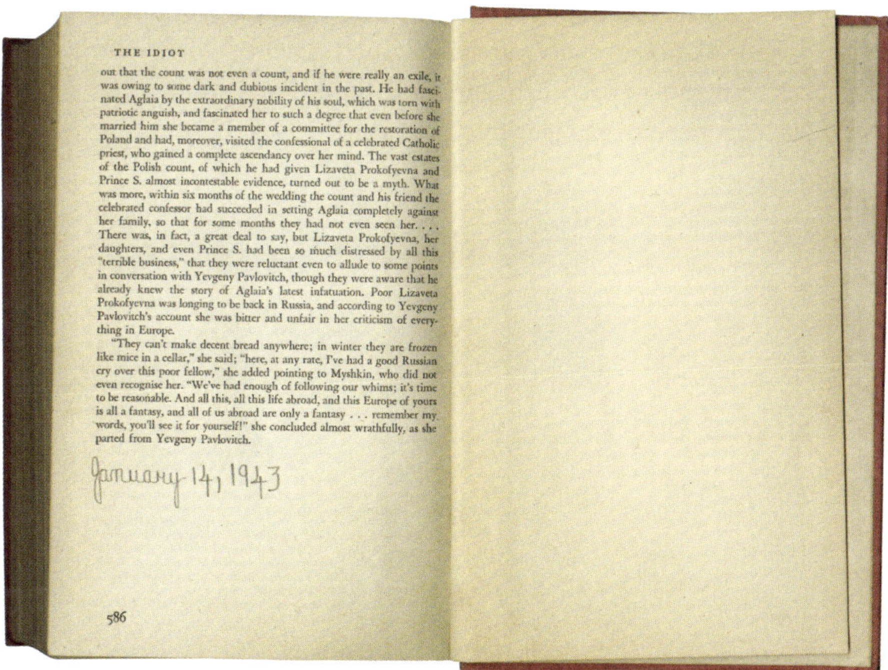

THE IDIOT

out that the count was not even a count, and if he were really an exile, it was owing to some dark and dubious incident in the past. He had fascinated Aglaia by the extraordinary nobility of his soul, which was torn with patriotic anguish, and fascinated her to such a degree that even before she married him she became a member of a committee for the restoration of Poland and had, moreover, visited the confessional of a celebrated Catholic priest, who gained a complete ascendancy over her mind. The vast estates of the Polish count, of which he had given Lizaveta Prokofyevna and Prince S. almost incontestable evidence, turned out to be a myth. What was more, within six months of the wedding the count and his friend the celebrated confessor had succeeded in setting Aglaia completely against her family, so that for some months they had not even seen her. . . . There was, in fact, a great deal to say, but Lizaveta Prokofyevna, her daughters, and even Prince S. had been so much distressed by all this "terrible business," that they were reluctant even to allude to some points in conversation with Yevgeny Pavlovitch, though they were aware that he already knew the story of Aglaia's latest infatuation. Poor Lizaveta Prokofyevna was longing to be back in Russia, and according to Yevgeny Pavlovitch's account she was bitter and unfair in her criticism of everything in Europe.

"They can't make decent bread anywhere; in winter they are frozen like mice in a cellar," she said; "here, at any rate, I've had a good Russian cry over this poor fellow," she added pointing to Myshkin, who did not even recognise her. "We've had enough of following our whims; it's time to be reasonable. And all this, all this life abroad, and this Europe of yours is all a fantasy, and all of us abroad are only a fantasy . . . remember my words, you'll see it for yourself!" she concluded almost wrathfully, as she parted from Yevgeny Pavlovitch.

January 14, 1943

586

Figure 8.1 *Annotated Final Page from Dostoyevsky's* The Idiot

This reading and the war were always connected in my mind—that one of the freedoms he was fighting for was the freedom to read the way he read. When I contemplate his own amazing advancement, from the orphanage to receiving a PhD in entomology from Ohio State (interrupted by three years in the South Pacific), I attribute it to his capacity for voracious reading. He could take on anything.

I'll conclude this chapter with the ending of his article because I don't think I can improve on the eloquence of this twenty-six-year-old champion of reading:

> In conclusion, I'd like to say that I believe there is a place for free reading in the high school; a place that provides a class with a supervised study period; a study period relatively free of drill and exercises; a place that possesses a sympathetic supervisor; but mostly a place that contains an enlightened teacher . . . who criticizes a book only after it has been read, who is slow to condemn any book, who doesn't hold too tightly to the line between fiction and nonfiction. Yes, especially an enlightened teacher—one who can remember that Carnegie made the library public; that teachers need to make it free. (Newkirk 1941, 329)

A Final Reflection on Veteran's Day

On this Veteran's Day Friday, I'm momentarily confused to see our neighbors' children out playing. Normally at this time the school buses would be winding their way through the neighborhood. Clusters of parents would be gathering with their children and often their dogs—a real social event. The bus would lumber to a stop, lights flashing. Children would scramble into the bus, greeted by name by the driver. It always reminds me how important bus drivers are, the first contact with school each day. There would be final waves from bus windows and then the children would be off.

This act of separation is so common that we can forget how extraordinary it is—sending those we cherish off to be taught by others. It is testament to the belief that as important as home and family are, they are not enough. Children need the chance to develop what has been called an outward-facing sense of self, a public identity, built on relations with teachers, friends, custodians, and bus drivers.

What hopes ride with that bus! We hope that our children will be *known*, that their interests and emerging talents will be recognized and developed, that they will find friends, and that they will become citizens of the school. In the terms of this book, we hope they will be viewed not as empty vessels to be filled, but as already possessing funds of knowledge.

In June 2022, a teacher posted a photo of a final, year-ending interaction with one of her students. She took the stance of a basketball player in a defensive crouch, arms outstretched, and the student, a fourth grader, pretended to put on some fake moves to get by her. In the photo it looked like he was trying a spin move. It was an end-of-the day ritual they had. This was the last occasion in the school year when they could act it out—and she wanted that recorded.

In every school, in every classroom, these rituals of connection occur—off curriculum, but profoundly important: a secret fist bump, an exchange about Taylor Swift's new album, a moment of gloating about a Red Sox victory over the Yankees, a word of praise about a soccer win. None of this, of course, counts directly in any test scores, or is featured in a scope and sequence chart or on any list of competencies. But in these moments *the outside comes in*, the school is permeable to the loyalties and experiences of students. The fourth grader's passion for basketball is acknowledged in the hallway routine—more than that, it is shared by the teacher.

But not today.

Today we stop to recognize veterans. When I go to the food store, there will be an American Legion vet offering facsimile poppies, and I will put a few dollars in his plastic tub. The choice of the poppy was inspired by a poem written by a surgeon in World War I who was surprised to see them growing on some of the most devastated battlefields. Today my thoughts will turn to my father and his friends who fought in the next war. Sometimes I reread his letters, which occasionally strayed into politics, like this comment in an August 6, 1944, letter from New Guinea to my aunt Gertrude Fraas, advising her not to vote for Republican Thomas Dewey:

> The regularity of your letter writing makes me ashamed of not having written sooner. If I had written it would have been to complain about the beef you're raising—or, at least the amount of beef I am eating.
>
> Or I would have written about politics. Suggesting (subtly I hope) that you vote for Roosevelt. Because his opponent is for nothing, and against everything, his qualification for the Presidency consisting of a moustache (Something I've disliked ever since Hitler raised one), a baritone

> voice, and a desire to keep soldiers from voting. I hardly see in him the capability to deal with Churchill and Stalin. Such shrewd men can be handled only by a Roosevelt, or a Fraas, or some other good Dutchman.

He continues on what he could have written about and concludes:

> Or, I could have written about the weather: it is raining.
>
> So it is just as well I didn't write except, perhaps, to say that you are all very much in my thoughts.

I cannot read it without tears.

As I have already noted, there is a strange connection in our family between that war and reading. My dad reading Dostoevsky in the rainy jungles of New Guinea. I had been aware that the reading of comic books was also a common experience for GIs—Superman, Batman, and especially Captain America were wildly popular. This affection for comics led to their tremendous popularity after the war. But I was unaware of the extraordinary book reading during the war. Historically, reading and freedom have been connected: soldiers in the Revolutionary War read Thomas Paine's *Common Sense* in their miserably cold encampments. But it was in World War II that there was a huge organized effort to supply soldiers with books, chronicled in Molly Guptill Manning's *When Books Went to War* (2014).

The freedom to read became the vivid dividing line between Hitler's fascism and American democracy. Of course, there were the horrific Nazi book burnings, bibliocausts, in the 1930s. In countries that were taken over, there was comprehensive censorship—ten thousand titles were banned, including US authors Ernest Hemingway, Jack London, and John Dos Passos, not to mention any Jewish writer. The United States created posters depicting these book burnings and quoting Franklin Roosevelt: "Books cannot be killed by fire. People die, but books never die. No man and no force can put thought in a concentration camp forever."

When the United States entered the war, librarians across the country organized drives, part of the Victory Book Campaign, to collect books and send them to GIs. But soon the US government came to view book

Books cannot be killed by fire.
People die, but books never die. No man and no force can put thought in a concentration camp forever. No man and no force can take from the world the books that embody man's eternal fight against tyranny. In this war, we know, books are weapons.
Franklin D Roosevelt
BRODER
BOOKS ARE WEAPONS IN THE WAR OF IDEAS
FOR ADDITIONAL COPIES WRITE DIVISION OF PUBLIC INQUIRY, OFFICE OF WAR INFORMATION, WASHINGTON, D. C. SPECIFY O. W. I. NO. 7

reading as essential for soldiers, and the Army Special Services division began printing selected books in a special paperback form. These were not the handsome hardbacks that my dad received in New Guinea; they were specially designed paperbacks, small enough to fit in a back pocket. Some of them had binding at the top, so readers would flip, not turn, pages.

Between 1943 and 1947, approximately 122 million copies, including 1,300 titles, were sent to soldiers, ranging from established classics (Emerson's essays) to popular entertainment (Bob Hope, Zane Grey). Some books were especially popular and emerged from the war as American classics. One of these was Betty Smith's *A Tree Grows in Brooklyn*. Soldiers were so moved by the book that they wrote to Smith, and she responded personally and sometimes sent a photo. One of her readers carried that photo from Germany to Belgium until it was so frayed he had to write and ask for another. Another soldier wrote about his "dead heart," the way his feelings shut down after seeing his friends die in battle. Reading *A Tree Grows in Brooklyn* brought him back to life: "I can't explain the emotional reaction that took place. I only know that it happened and that this heart of mine turned over and became alive again" (Manning 2014, xi–xii).

Another book that emerged as a classic was *The Great Gatsby*, which by publishing standards had been a failure before the war, selling only twenty thousand copies when it first came out in 1925. Fitzgerald died in 1940 thinking the book would be forgotten. But it was a tremendous hit with soldiers. Over the four years in which the American Service Editions were distributed, 155,000 copies of *Gatsby* were sent. Soldiers passed these books around, and by some estimates, each copy was read about seven times, which would equate to over a million readers. It is a fantastic fact that *Gatsby* was rescued from obscurity not by literary critics, but by soldiers hardly older than students who read it in schools today.

Books and freedom are inevitably intertwined. It's no coincidence that in Latin the word for book and freedom is identical—*liber*. It also refers to the Roman god of wine and fertility (hence, *libertine*). Thus our words *library* and *liberty* have the same root. Reading is an open system in which no one can fully predict or control the transaction. As

As readers we are not confined in the four corners of the text. We bring our prior experience, our biases, our values, our practical theories of human behavior—and put them to a test. We act and are acted upon.

readers we are not confined in the four corners of the text. We bring our prior experience, our biases, our values, our practical theories of human behavior—and put them to a test. We act and are acted upon. We encounter something different and need to be open to that difference, and open to being affected, even changed by it. To stay with etymology, our very word *novel* comes from the same word in old French, later *nouvelle*—"new."

The emotional chemistry of this transaction is hard to predict—who could have imagined the soldiers mired in the brutal European winter of 1944–45 would be so drawn to Gatsby and East Egg? Did they connect to the feelings of longing, of hope deferred? That green light? I imagine that some of these battered copies, soiled with mud from trenches in the Ardennes forests, were in the duffels of returning soldiers, passing the Statue of Liberty and in view of Manhattan, where so much of the novel occurred. It is night, and the city is brilliantly illuminated. I imagine those soldiers on deck, leaning against the railing for a good view.

What they must have felt.

—November 11, 2022

REFERENCES

INTRODUCTION: Literacy and Democracy—or "Where I'm From"

Addams, Jane. 1908. "The Public School and the Immigrant Child." *Journal of Proceedings of the National Education Association* 46: 99–102.

Cremin, Lawrence. 1961. *The Transformation of the School: Progressivism in American Education 1876–1957*. New York: Vintage.

Dewey, John. 1910. *How We Think*. Boston: D. C. Heath.

———. 1938. *Experience and Education*. New York: Touchstone.

———. 1900/1956. *The Child and the Curriculum* and *The School and Society*. Chicago: University of Chicago Press.

Dickens, Charles. 2003. *Hard Times*. New York: Penguin.

Dweck, Carol. 2006. *Mindset: The New Psychology of Success*. New York: Ballantine Books.

Dyson, Anne Haas. 1993. *Social Worlds of Children Learning to Write in an Urban Primary School*. New York: Teachers College Press.

Freire, Paulo. 1970. *Pedagogy of the Oppressed*. New York: Bloomsbury Academic.

Johnston, Peter. 2004. *Choice Words: How Our Language Affects Children's Learning*. Portland, ME: Stenhouse.

Macrotrends. 2010–23. "U.S. GDP Growth Rate 1961–2023." Macrotrends (website). https://www.macrotrends.net/countries/USA/united-states/gdp-growth-rate.

Menand, Louis. 2001. *The Metaphysical Club: A Story of Ideas in America*. New York: Farrar, Straus and Giroux.

Miller, Debbie, and Emily Callahan. 2022. *I'm the Kind of Kid Who . . . : Invitations That Support Learner Identity and Agency.* Portsmouth, NH: Heinemann.

Montaigne, Michel de. 1958. *Essays*. Translated by J. M. Cohen. New York: Penguin.

———. 1987. *The Complete Essays*. Translated by M. A. Screech. New York: Penguin.

National Commission on Excellence in Education. 1983. *A Nation at Risk: The Imperative for Educational Reform*. Washington, DC: Department of Education.

Putnam, Robert D., with Shaylyn Romney Garrett. 2020. *The Upswing: How America Came Together a Century Ago and How We Can Do It Again.* New York: Simon and Schuster.

Rousseau, Jean-Jacques. 1979. *Emile, or On Education*. Translated by Allan Bloom. New York: Basic Books.

Tatum, Alfred W. 2009. *Reading for Their Life: (Re)Building the Textual Lineages of African American Adolescent Males.* Portsmouth, NH: Heinemann.

Upchurch, Carl. 1996. *Convicted in the Womb: One Man's Journey from Prisoner to Peacemaker.* New York: Bantam.

Volinsky, Andru H. 2004. "New Hampshire's Education-Funding Litigation: *Claremont School District v. Governor*, 635 A.2d 1375 (N.H. 1993), *modified*, 703 A.2d 1353 (N.H. 1997)." *Nebraska Law Review* 83 (3): 836–55.

Whitehead, Alfred North. 1967. *The Aims of Education and Other Essays*. New York: Free Press.

Willingham, Daniel T. 2006. "How Knowledge Helps: It Speeds and Strengthens Reading Comprehension, Learning—and Thinking." *American Educator* 30 (1): 30–37. https://www.aft.org/periodical/american-educator/spring-2006/how-knowledge-helps.

CHAPTER ONE: Expressive Language

Bartholomae, David. 1983. "Writing Assignments: Where Writing Begins." In *FFORUM: Essays on Theory and Practice in the Teaching of Writing*, edited by Patricia Stock, 300–12. Upper Montclair, NJ: Boynton/Cook.

Brande, Dorothea. 1934. *Becoming a Writer.* New York: Harcourt, Brace.

Britton, James. 1982. "Shaping at the Point of Utterance." In *Prospect and Retrospect: Selected Essays of James Britton*, edited by Gordon Pradl, 139–45. Montclair, NJ: Boynton/Cook.

Britton, James, Tony Burgess, Nancy Martin, Alex McLeod, and Harold Rosen. 1975. *The Development of Writing Abilities (11–18).* London: Macmillan.

Carpenter, George R., Franklin T. Baker, and Fred N. Scott. 1903. *The Teaching of English in the Elementary and Secondary School.* New York: Longmans, Green.

Christensen, Francis. 1963. "A Generative Rhetoric of the Sentence." *College Composition and Communication* 14 (3): 155–61.

Elbow, Peter. 1973. *Writing Without Teachers*. New York: Oxford University Press.

———. 2012. *Vernacular Eloquence: What Speech Can Bring to Writing*. New York: Oxford University Press.

———. 2022. Personal interview. September 12.

Heller, Nathan. 2021. "Comment: Recall Fever." *New Yorker* (September 6): 13–14.

Holt-Shannon, Mark. 2019. Personal interview. September 24.

Mehan, Hugh. 2014. *Learning Lessons: Social Organization in the Classroom*. Cambridge: Harvard University Press.

Melville, Herman. 2018. *Moby Dick*. Scotts Valley, CA: CreateSpace.

Murray, Donald. 1982. "Listening to Writing." In *Learning by Teaching: Selected Articles on Writing and Teaching*, 53–65. Montclair, NJ: Boynton/Cook.

Rief, Linda. 2018. *The Quickwrite Handbook: 100 Mentor Texts to Jumpstart Your Students' Thinking and Writing*. Portsmouth, NH: Heinemann.

Shaughnessy, Mina. 1977. *Errors and Expectations: A Guide for the Teacher of Basic Writing*. New York: Oxford University Press.

Simic, Charles. 1994. "Food and Happiness." In *The Unemployed Fortune-Teller: Essays and Memoirs*, 6–12. Ann Arbor: University of Michigan Press.

Sterne, Laurence. 2003. *The Life and Opinions of Tristram Shandy, Gentleman*. New York: Penguin.

Vygotsky, Lev S. 1962. *Thought and Language*. Translated by Eugenia Hanfmann and Gertrude Vakar. Cambridge, MA: The MIT Press.

———. 1978. *Mind in Society: The Development of Higher Psychological Processes*. Cambridge: Harvard University Press.

Woolf, Virginia. 1989. *To the Lighthouse*. New York: Harcourt Brace Jovanovich.

CHAPTER TWO: **Funds of Knowledge**

Amanti, Cathy. 2005. "Beyond a Beads and Feathers Approach." In *Funds of Knowledge: Theorizing Practices in Households, Communities, and Classrooms*, edited by Norma González, Luis C. Moll, and Cathy Amanti, 131–41. Mahwah, NJ: Erlbaum.

Coleman, David. 2012. "Bringing the Common Core to Life." T F, March 2. YouTube video, 0:37. https://www.youtube.com/watch?v=Pu6lin88YXU.

Dyson, Anne Haas. 1993. *Negotiating a Permeable Curriculum: On Literacy, Diversity, and the Interplay of Children's and Teacher's Worlds*. NCTE Concept Paper no. 9. Urbana, IL: NCTE.

———. 2001. "Coach Bombay's Kids Learn to Write: Children's Appropriation of Media Material for School Literacy." In *Literacy: A Critical Sourcebook*, edited by Ellen Cushman, Eugene R. Kintgen, Barry M. Kroll, and Mike Rose, 325–57. Boston: Bedford.

———. 2003. *The Brothers and Sisters Learn to Write: Popular Literacies in Childhood and School Cultures*. New York: Teachers College Press.

Eodice, Michele, Anne Ellen Geller, and Neal Lerner. 2019. "The Power of Personal Connection for Undergraduate Student Writers." *Research in the Teaching of English* 53 (4): 320–39.

Germán, Lorena Escoto. 2021. *Textured Teaching: A Framework for Culturally Sustaining Practices*. Portsmouth, NH: Heinemann.

Gladwell, Malcolm. 2011. *Outliers: The Story of Success*. Little, Brown.

Herrington, Anne J., and Marcia Curtis. 2000. *Persons in Process: Four Stories of Writing and Personal Development in College*. Urbana, IL: NCTE.

Ladson-Billings, Gloria. 1995. "But That's Just Good Teaching! The Case for Culturally Relevant Pedagogy." *Theory into Practice* 34 (3): 159–65.

Lander, Jessica. 2022. "Creating Classrooms That Draw on Immigrants' Skills." *The Boston Globe*, November 22: A11.

Melzer, Dan. 2014. *Assignments Across the Curriculum: A National Study of College Writing*. Logan: Utah State University Press.

Moll, Luis C. 2014. *Vygotsky and Education: Instructional Implications and Applications of Sociohistorical Psychology*. New York: Routledge.

Moll, Luis C., Cathy Amanti, Deborah Neff, and Norma González. 1992. "Funds of Knowledge for Teaching: Using a Qualitative Approach to Connect Homes and Classrooms." *Theory into Practice* 31 (2): 132–41.

Muhammad, Gholdy. 2020. *Cultivating Genius: An Equity Framework for Culturally and Historically Responsive Literacy*. New York: Scholastic.

National Governors Association (NGA) Center for Best Practices and Council of Chief State School Officers (CCSSO). 2010. *Common Core State Standards for English Language Arts and Literacy in History/Social Studies, Science, and Technical Subjects: Appendix A: Research Supporting Key Elements of the Standards*. Washington, DC: NGA Center for Best Practices and CCSSO.

Rossi, Ginette. 2022. Personal interview. August 26.

Tatum, Alfred. 2009. *Reading for Their Life: (Re)Building the Textual Lineages of African American Adolescent Males*. Portsmouth, NH: Heinemann.

Thaiss, Christopher, and Terry Myers Zawacki. 2006. *Engaged Writers and Dynamic Disciplines: Research on the Academic Writing Life*. Portsmouth, NH: Boynton/Cook.

Vygotsky, Lev S. 1962. *Thought and Language*. Cambridge: MIT Press.

Wilhelm, Jeffrey. 2013. *Deepening Comprehension with Action Strategies: Role Plays, Text-Structure Tableaux, Talking Statues, and Other Enactment Techniques That Engage Students with Text*. 2nd ed., including DVD. New York: Scholastic.

Yosso, Tara J. 2005. "Whose Culture Has Capital? A Critical Race Theory Discussion of Community Cultural Wealth." *Race Ethnicity and Education* 8 (1): 69–91.

CHAPTER THREE: Transactional Model of Reading

Atwell, Nancie. 2015. *In the Middle: A Lifetime of Learning About Writing, Reading, and Adolescents*. 3rd ed. Portsmouth, NH: Heinemann.

Atwell, Nancie, and Anne Atwell Merkel. 2009. *The Reading Zone: How to Help Kids Become Passionate, Skilled, Habitual, Critical Readers*. New York: Scholastic.

Bartholomae, David, and Anthony Petrosky. 2011. *Ways of Reading: An Anthology for Writers*. 9th ed. Boston: Bedford/St. Martin's.

Beers, Kylene, and Robert E. Probst. 2014. *Notice & Note: Strategies for Close Reading*. Portsmouth, NH: Heinemann.

———. 2016. *Reading Nonfiction: Notice & Note: Stances, Signposts, and Strategies*. Portsmouth, NH: Heinemann.

Coleman, David, and Susan Pimentel. 2012. *Revised Publishers' Criteria for the Common Core State Standards in English Language Arts and Literacy, Grades 3–12*. Washington, DC: NGA Center for Best Practices and CCSSO. National Science Teachers Association (website). https://static.nsta.org/pdfs/2013CongressCCSSFor3-12.pdf.

Dewey, John. 1934. *Art as Experience*. New York: Perigee Books.

Egan, Jennifer. 2010. *A Visit from the Goon Squad*. New York: Knopf.

Fitzgerald, F. Scott. 1995. *The Great Gatsby*. New York: Scribner's.

Kenyon, Jane. 1990. "Let Evening Come." In *Let Evening Come*. Minneapolis, MN: Graywolf.

Kittle, Penny. 2010. "Why Students Don't Read What Is Assigned in Class." Heinemann, March 15. YouTube video, 5:28. https://www.youtube.com/watch?v=gokm9RUr4ME.

Lindberg, Gary. 1986. "Coming to Words." In *Only Connect: Uniting Reading and Writing*, edited by Thomas Newkirk, 143–57. Upper Montclair, NJ: Boynton/Cook.

Montaigne, Michel de. 1987. *The Complete Essays*. Translated by M. A. Screech. New York: Penguin.

Plato. 2005. *Phaedrus*. New York: Penguin.

Probst, Robert E. 1988. *Response and Analysis: Teaching Literature in Junior and Senior High School*. Portsmouth, NH: Boynton/Cook.

———. 2022. Personal interview. January 7.

Richards, I. A. 1929. *Practical Criticism: A Study of Literary Judgment*. New York: Harcourt, Brace.

Rosenblatt, Louise. 1978. *The Reader, the Text, and the Poem: The Transactional Theory of the Literary Work*. Carbondale: Southern Illinois University Press.

Seneca. 1969. *Letters from a Stoic*. Translated by Robin Campbell. New York: Penguin.

Scholes, Robert. 1982. *Semiotics and Interpretation*. New Haven, CT: Yale University Press.

Wilhelm, Jeffrey D. 1996. *"You Gotta BE the Book": Teaching Engaged and Reflective Reading with Adolescents*. New York: Teachers College Press.

Wilhelm, Jeffrey D., and Michael W. Smith with Sharon Fransen. 2014. *Reading Unbound: Why Kids Need to Read What They Want—and Why We Should Let Them*. New York: Scholastic.

Wilson, Maja, and Thomas Newkirk. 2011. "Can Readers Really Stay Within the Standards Lines?" *Education Week*, December 13. https://www.edweek.org/teaching-learning/opinion-can-readers-really-stay-within-the-standards-lines/2011/12.

Wimsatt, W. K., Jr., and Monroe C. Beardsley. 1949. "The Affective Fallacy." *The Sewanee Review* 57 (1): 31–55.

Woolf, Virginia. 1925. *The Common Reader*. First series. New York: Harcourt, Brace. https://www.gutenberg.org/cache/epub/64457/pg64457-images.html.

CHAPTER FOUR: The Writing Process

Atwell, Nancie. 2022. Personal interview. March 25.

Barbieri, Maureen. 2022. Personal communication.

Beckett, Andy. 1996. "A Career Written in Blood." *The Independent*, March 10: 19.

Brandt, Deborah. 2015. *The Rise of Writing: Redefining Mass Literacy*. Cambridge: Cambridge University Press.

Dweck, Carol. 2006. *Mindset: The Psychology of Success*. New York: Ballantine.

Elbow, Peter. 1973. *A Writer Teaches Writing*. New York: Oxford.

Gilb, Dagoberto. 1999. "Victoria." In *The Best American Essays, 1999*, edited by Edward Hoagland, 105–10. Boston: Houghton Mifflin.

Gladwell, Malcolm. 2011. *Outliers: The Story of Success*. Boston: Little, Brown.

Graves, Donald. 1978/2013. "Balance the Basics: Let Them Write." In *Children Want to Write: Donald Graves and the Revolution in Children's Writing*, edited by Thomas Newkirk and Penny Kittle, 20–37. Portsmouth: Heinemann.

———. 1983. *Writing: Teachers and Children at Work*. Portsmouth, NH: Heinemann.

Hall, Chris. 2021. *The Writer's Mindset: 6 Stances That Promote Authentic Revision*. Portsmouth, NH: Heinemann.

Johnston, Peter. 2004. *Choice Words: How Our Language Affects Children's Learning*. Portland, ME: Stenhouse.

Keene, Ellin Oliver. 2022. *The Literacy Studio: Redesigning the Workshop for Readers and Writers*. Portsmouth, NH: Heinemann.

Murray, Donald. 1982. "Teaching the Other Self: The Writer's First Reader." In *Learning by Teaching: Selected Articles on Writing and Teaching*, 164–72. Montclair, NJ: Boynton/Cook.

———. 1984. *A Writer Teaches Writing*. 2nd ed. Boston: Houghton Mifflin.

Newkirk, Thomas. 1988. "Young Writers as Critical Readers." In *Understanding Writing: Ways of Observing, Learning, and Teaching K–8*, edited by Thomas Newkirk and Nancie Atwell, 154–60. Portsmouth, NH: Heinemann.

———. 2021. *Writing Unbound: How Fiction Transforms Student Writers*. Portsmouth, NH: Heinemann.

Pearson, David, and Margaret Gallagher. 1983. "The Instruction of Reading Comprehension." *Contemporary Educational Psychology* 8 (3): 317–44.

Perl, Sondra. 1980. "Understanding Composing." *College Composition and Communication* 31 (4): 363–69.

———. 2015. "Oral History of Teaching Writing at City University in the 1970s." Comp Comm, November 14. YouTube video, 31:29. https://www.youtube.com/watch?v=9O3iNLstTiQ.

———. 2022. Personal interview. March 9.

Prather, Liz. 2022. *The Confidence to Write: A Guide for Overcoming Fear and Developing Identity as a Writer*. Portsmouth, NH: Heinemann.

Prather, Liz, and Thomas Newkirk. 2022. "Abandoning the Myth of the Master Writer." *Heinemann Podcast*, March 3. https://blog.heinemann.com/podcast-abandoning-the-myth-master-writer-liz-prather-tom-newkirk.

Ray, Katie Wood. 1999. *Wondrous Words: Writers and Writing in the Elementary Classroom*. Urbana, IL: NCTE.

———. 2022. Personal interview. March 3.

Shaughnessy, Mina. 1977. *Errors and Expectations: A Guide for the Teacher of Basic Writing*. New York: Oxford University Press.

Sheils, Merrill. 1975. "Why Johnny Can't Write." *Newsweek*, December 8: 58–65.

Van Allen, Roach, and Claryce Allen. 1982. *Language Experience Activities*. 2d ed. Boston: Houghton Mifflin.

CHAPTER FIVE: **Translanguaging**

Abojaradeh, Lina. 2017. "I Am Limitless—Poem on Identity." Lina Abojaradeh, March 12. YouTube video, 1:52. https://www.youtube.com/watch?v=f5CLnmN2QcQ.

Anzaldúa, Gloria. 1987. *Borderlands/La Frontera: The New Mestiza*. San Francisco: Aunt Lute.

Cisneros, Sandra. 1983. *The House on Mango Street*. Houston: Arte Publico.

Cummins, Jim. 2000. *Language, Power, and Pedagogy: Bilingual Children in the Crossfire*. Clevedon, UK: Multilingual Matters.

Delpit, Lisa. 2006. *Other People's Children: Cultural Conflict in the Classroom*. New York: New Press.

Díaz, Junot. 1996. *Drown*. New York: Riverhead Books.

Dwyer, Dialynn. 2022. "Watch: Ketanji Brown Jackson Shares the Message She Received from a Stranger in Harvard Yard." Boston .com, March 24. https://www.boston.com/news/politics/2022/03/24 /ketanji-brown-jackson-harvard-yard-persevere/.

Early, Jessica Singer. 2022. *Next Generation Genres: Teaching Writing for Civic and Academic Engagement*. New York: Norton.

España, Carla, and Luz Yadira Herrara. 2020. *En Comunidad: Lessons for Centering the Voices and Experiences of Bilingual Latinx Students*. Portsmouth, NH: Heinemann.

Fernandes, Marino Ivo Lopes, Alicia Clark-Barnes, and Christina Ortmeier-Hooper. 2022. "Units of Exchange: How Teachers Develop Assignments with Academic Currency for Plurilingual Identities." In *Plurilingual Pedagogies for Multilingual Writing Classrooms*, edited by Kay Losey and Gail Shuck, 75–91. New York: Routledge.

Fu, Danling. 2007. "Teaching Writing to English Language Learners." In *Teaching the Neglected "R": Rethinking Writing Instruction in Secondary Classrooms*, edited by Thomas Newkirk and Richard Kent, 225–42. Portsmouth, NH: Heinemann.

———. 2022. Personal interview. August 24.

Fu, Danling, Xenia Hadjioannou, and Xiaodi Zhou. 2019. *Translanguaging for Emergent Bilinguals: Inclusive Teaching in the Linguistically Diverse Classroom*. New York: Teachers College Press.

García, Ofelia. 2009. *Bilingual Education in the 21st Century: A Global Perspective*. Malden, MA: Wiley-Blackwell.

García, Ofelia, and Jo Anne Kleifgen. 2019. "Translanguaging and Literacies." *Reading Research Quarterly* 55 (4): 553–71.

Grady, Denise. 1993. "The Vision Thing: Mainly in the Brain." *Discover*, June 1. https://www.discovermagazine.com/mind /the-vision-thing-mainly-in-the-brain.

Heath, Shirley Brice. 1983. *Ways with Words: Language, Life and Work in Communities and Classrooms*. Cambridge: Cambridge University Press.

Latino Book Review. 2017. "Ten Bilingual Poetry Books for National Poetry Month." Latino Book Review (website), April 20. https://www.latinobookreview.com/10-bilingual-poetry-books-to-read-during-national-poetry-month.html.

Lyon, George Ella. n.d. "Where I'm From." Smithsonian (website). https://smithsonianeducation.org/educators/professional_development/workshops/writing/george_ella_lyon.pdf.

Matam, Pages, Elizabeth Acevedo, and G. Yamazawa. 2014. "NPS 2014 Semi-Finals—Beltway—G. Yamazawa, Liz Acevedo, Pages Matam 'Unforgettable.'" Poetry Slam Inc, December 4. YouTube video, 3:05. https://www.youtube.com/watch?v=FUKDivyfvFY.

Méndez, Yamile Saied. 2020. *Furia*. Chapel Hill, NC: Algonquin Young Readers.

Muhammad, Gholdy. 2020. *Cultivating Genius: An Equity Framework for Culturally and Historically Responsive Literacy*. New York: Scholastic.

Oakes, Jeanine. 2005. *Keeping Track: How Schools Structure Inequality*. 2nd ed. New Haven, CT: Yale University Press.

Ortmeier-Hooper, Christina. 2013. *The ELL Writer: Moving Beyond Basics in the Secondary Classroom*. New York: Teachers College Press.

Philips, Susan U. 1972. "Participant Structures and Communicative Competence: Warm Springs Children in Community and Classroom." In *Functions of Language in the Classroom*, edited by Courtney B. Cazden, Vera P. John, and Dell Hymes, 370–94. New York: Teachers College Press.

Rodriguez, Richard. 1983. *Hunger of Memory: The Education of Richard Rodriguez*. New York: Bantam.

Schlesinger, Arthur M., Jr. 1991. *The Disuniting of America: Reflections on a Multicultural Society*. New York: W. W. Norton.

Statista Research Department. 2023. "The Most Spoken Languages Worldwide in 2022." Statista (website), March 31. https://www.statista.com/statistics/266808/the-most-spoken-languages-worldwide/.

CHAPTER SIX: **Story**

Adichie, Chimamanda Ngozi. 2009. "The Danger of a Single Story." Filmed July 2009 in Oxford, England. TED video, 18:33. https://www.ted.com/talks/chimamanda_ngozi_adichie_the_danger_of_a_single_story/comments.

Bartholomae, David. 1983. "Writing Assignments: Where Writing Begins." In *FForum: Essays on Theory and Practice in the Teaching of Writing*, edited by Patricia Stock, 300–12. Upper Montclair, NJ: Boynton/Cook.

Booth, Wayne. 1963. "The Rhetorical Stance." *College Composition and Communication* 14 (3): 139–45.

Desmond, Matthew. 2017. *Evicted: Poverty and Profit in the American City*. New York: Broadway Books.

Elbow, Peter. 1973. *Writing Without Teachers*. New York: Oxford University Press.

———. 2012. *Vernacular Eloquence: What Speech Can Bring to Writing*. New York: Oxford University Press.

Goody, Jack. 1977. *The Domestication of the Savage Mind*. Cambridge: Cambridge University Press.

Graff, Gerald, and Cathy Birkenstein. 2021. *They Say/I Say: The Moves That Matter in Academic Writing*. 5th ed. New York: W. W. Norton.

Kahneman, Daniel. 2011. *Thinking, Fast and Slow*. New York: Farrar, Straus and Giroux.

Kinneavy, James. 1971. *A Theory of Discourse: The Aims of Discourse.* Englewood Cliffs, NJ: Prentice Hall.

Lee, Harper. 1960. *To Kill a Mockingbird.* New York: Harper Collins.

Lunsford, Andrea. 1979. "Cognitive Development and the Basic Writer." *College English* 41 (1): 38–46.

Mueller, Lisel. 1980 "Why We Tell Stories." In *The Need to Hold Still.* Baton Rouge, LA: LSU Press.

Murray, Donald. 2004. *The Craft of Revision.* 5th ed. Fort Worth, TX: Harcourt.

Newkirk, Thomas. 1987. "The Non-narrative Writing of Young Children." *Research in the Teaching of English* 21 (2): 121–44.

———. 2013. *Minds Made for Stories: How We Really Read and Write Informational and Persuasive Texts.* Portsmouth, NH: Heinemann.

Nielsen, Jakob. 2006. "F-Shaped Pattern for Reading Web Content (Original Study)." Nielsen Norman Group (website), April 16. https://www.nngroup.com/articles/f-shaped-pattern-reading-web-content-discovered/.

Pinker, Steven. 2014. *The Sense of Style: The Thinking Person's Guide to Writing in the 21st Century.* New York: Viking.

Turner, Mark. 1996. *The Literary Mind.* New York: Oxford University Press.

Ulrich, Laurel Thatcher. 1991. *A Midwife's Tale: The Life of Martha Ballard, Based on Her Diary, 1785–1812.* New York: Viking.

Willingham, Daniel. 2004. "The Privileged Status of Story." *American Educator* (Summer). https://www.aft.org/periodical/american-educator/summer-2004/ask-cognitive-scientist.

Wilson, William Julius. 1997. *When Work Disappears: The World of the New Urban Poor.* New York: Vintage.

CHAPTER SEVEN: **Multi (Multimodal, Multiliteracies, Multigenre)**

Atkins, Anna. 1843. *Photographs of British Algae: Cyanotype Impressions*. n.p.: Printed by the author.

Auster, Paul. 1995. *Smoke*. Movie script. Scripts.com. https://www.scripts.com/script-pdf/739.

Ballenger, Bruce. 2001. "Learning to Trust the Twelfth Picture on the Roll." In *The Subject Is Research*, edited by Wendy Bishop, 29–42. Portsmouth, NH: Heinemann.

Black Youth Project contributors. 2011. "Spoken Word Poetry: Hold onto That History." Black Youth Project (website), October 25. http://blackyouthproject.com/spoken-word-poetry-hold-onto-that-history/.

Carr, Nicholas. 2010. *The Shallows: How the Internet Is Changing the Way We Think, Read, and Remember*. London: Atlantic Books.

Coppola, Shawna. 2020. *Writing Redefined: Broadening Our Ideas of What It Means to Compose*. Portsmouth, NH: Stenhouse.

Defoe, Daniel. 1920. *Robinson Crusoe*. New York: Scribner's.

Dyson, Anne Haas. 1993. *Social Worlds of Children Learning to Write in an Urban Primary School*. New York: Teachers College Press.

Grandin, Temple. 2023. "Society Is Failing Visual Thinkers: And That Hurts Us All." *New York Times*, January 9. https://www.nytimes.com/2023/01/09/opinion/temple-grandin-visual-thinking-autism.html.

Hobbs, Renee, Denise Chapman, Candance M. Doerr-Stevens, Seth D. French, Tom Liam Lynch, Cruz Medina, Ernest Morrell, Chris Sloan, Lisa Stringfellow, and Kristin Ziemke. 2022. "Media Education in the English Language Arts." National Council of Teachers of English (website), April 9. https://ncte.org/statement/media_education/.

Horn, Martha, and Mary Ellen Giacobbe. 2007. *Talking, Drawing, Writing: Lessons for Our Youngest Writers*. Portland, ME: Stenhouse.

Kittle, Penny, and Kelly Gallagher. 2021. *4 Essential Studies: Beliefs and Practices to Reclaim Student Agency.* Portsmouth, NH: Heinemann.

Kress, Gunther R. 2010. *Multimodality: A Social Semiotic Approach to Contemporary Communication*. New York: Routledge.

LaVallee, Laura. 2022. Personal interview. October 3.

Leander, Kevin, and Gail Boldt. 2013. "Rereading 'A Pedagogy of Multiliteracies': Bodies, Texts, and Emergence." *Journal of Literacy Research* 45 (1): 22–46.

Molano, Sarah. 2021. "Youth Depression and Anxiety Doubled During the Pandemic, New Analysis Finds." CNN (website), August 10. https://www.cnn.com/2021/08/10/health/covid-child-teen-depression-anxiety-wellness/index.html.

Moll, Luis C. 2014. *Vygotsky and Education: Instructional Implications and Applications of Sociohistorical Psychology*. New York: Routledge.

New London Group. 1996. "A Pedagogy of Multiliteracies: Designing Social Futures." *Harvard Educational Review* 66 (1): 60–92.

Newkirk, Thomas. 2021. *Writing Unbound: How Fiction Transforms Student Writers*. Portsmouth, NH: Heinemann.

Ondaatje, Michael. 1970. *The Collected Works of Billy the Kid*. New York: Vintage.

Pennebaker, James W., and John F. Evans. 2014. *Expressive Writing: Words That Heal.* Bedford, IN: Idyll Arbor.

Postman, Neil. 1979. *Teaching as a Conserving Activity.* New York: Dell.

Racine, Nicole, Brae Anne McArthur, Jessica E. Cooke, Rachel Eirich, Jenney Zhu, and Sheri Madigan. 2021. "Global Prevalence of Depressive and Anxiety Symptoms in Children and Adolescents During COVID-19: A Meta-analysis." *JAMA Pediatrics* 175 (11): 1142–50. https://jamanetwork.com/journals/jamapediatrics/fullarticle/2782796.

Romano, Tom. 2000. *Blending Genre, Altering Style: Writing Multigenre Papers*. Portsmouth, NH: Heinemann.

Schmoker, Mike. 2022. "No, Fewer Books, Less Writing Won't Add Up to Media Literacy." *Education Week*, June 3. https://www.edweek.org/teaching-learning/opinion-no-fewer-books-less-writing-wont-add-up-to-media-literacy/2022/06.

Trillin, Calvin. 1984. "The Best Restaurants in the World." In *The Contemporary Essay*, edited by Donald Hall, 377–89. Boston: Bedford/St. Martin's.

Turkle, Sherry. 2016. *Reclaiming Conversation: The Power of Talk in a Digital Age*. New York: Penguin.

Wolf, Maryanne. 2018. *Reader, Come Home: The Reading Brain in a Digital World*. New York: Harper.

CHAPTER EIGHT: **Independent Reading**

Addams, Jane. 1908. "The Public School and the Immigrant Child." *Journal of Proceedings of the National Education Association* 46: 99–102.

American Library Association. 2020. "Top 100 Most Banned and Challenged Books: 2010–2019." Banned and Challenged Books, September 9. https://www.ala.org/advocacy/bbooks/frequentlychallengedbooks/decade2019.

Anderson, Carl. 2000. *How's It Going? A Practical Guide to Conferring with Student Writers*. Portsmouth, NH: Heinemann.

Applebee, Arthur. 1974. *Tradition and Reform in the Teaching of English: A History*. Urbana, IL: NCTE.

Atwell, Nancie. 1987. *In the Middle: Writing, Reading, and Learning with Adolescents*. Upper Montclair, NJ: Boynton/Cook.

———. 2015. *In the Middle: A Lifetime of Learning About Writing, Reading, and Adolescents*. 3rd ed. Portsmouth, NH: Heinemann.

———. 2022. Personal interview. March 25.

Atwell, Nancie, and Anne Atwell Merkel. 2009. *The Reading Zone: How to Help Kids Become Passionate, Skilled, Habitual, Critical Readers*. New York: Scholastic.

Cullinan, Bernice E. 2000. "Independent Reading and School Achievement." *School Library Media Research* 3: 1–24. https://www.ala.org/aasl/sites/ala.org.aasl/files/content/aaslpubsandjournals/slr/vol3/SLMR_IndependentReading_V3.pdf.

Daoud, Kamel. 2015. "Insolence, Exile, and the Kingdom: Robert Zaretsky Interviews Kamel Daoud." Interview by Robert Zaretsky. *Los Angeles Review of Books*, June 9. https://lareviewofbooks.org/article/insolence-exile-and-the-kingdom/.

Ebarvia, Tricia, Lorena Germán, Kimberly N. Parker, and Julia Torres. 2020. "#DisruptTexts: An Introduction." *English Journal* 110 (1): 100–02.

Gallagher, Kelly, and Penny Kittle. 2018. *180 Days: Two Teachers and the Quest to Engage and Empower Adolescents*. Portsmouth, NH: Heinemann.

Hansen, Jane. 1987. *When Writers Read*. Portsmouth, NH: Heinemann.

Ivey, Gay, and Peter H. Johnston. 2013. "Engagement with Young Adult Literature: Outcomes and Processes." *Reading Research Quarterly* 48 (3): 255–75.

Jensen, Julie, ed. 1984. *Composing and Comprehending*. Urbana, IL: NCTE.

Keats, John. 1899. *The Complete Poetical Works and Letters of John Keats*. Cambridge ed. Boston: Houghton, Mifflin.

Keene, Ellin Oliver. 2022. *The Literacy Studio: Reimagining the Workshop for Readers and Writers*. Portsmouth, NH: Heinemann.

King, Stephen. 1981. *Cujo*. New York: Viking.

Kittle, Penny. 2010. "Why Students Don't Read What Is Assigned in Class." Heinemann, March 15. YouTube video, 5:28. https://www.youtube.com/watch?v=gokm9RUr4ME.

———. 2012. *Book Love: Developing Depth, Stamina, and Passion in Adolescent Readers*. Portsmouth, NH: Heinemann.

———. Personal interview. June 7.

McGuffey, William H. 1879. *McGuffey's Fifth Eclectic Reader*. Rev. ed. Cincinnati and New York: Van Antwerp, Bragg.

Miller, Debbie, and Barbara Moss. 2013. *No More Independent Reading Without Support*. Portsmouth, NH: Heinemann.

National Governors Association (NGA) Center for Best Practices and Council of Chief State School Officers (CCSSO). 2010. *Common Core State Standards for English Language Arts and Literacy in History/Social Studies, Science, and Technical Subjects*. Washington, DC: NGA Center for Best Practices and CCSSO. https://learning.ccsso.org/wp-content/uploads/2022/11/ELA_Standards1.pdf.

National Reading Panel. 2000. *Report of the National Reading Panel: Teaching Children to Read*. Washington, DC: National Institutes of Health.

Newkirk, Maurice. 1941. "A Venture into Free Reading." *Ohio Schools* (October): 328–29.

Newkirk, Thomas. 2021. *Writing Unbound: How Fiction Transforms Student Writers*. Portsmouth, NH: Heinemann.

Rideout, Victoria J., Ulla G. Foehr, and Donald F. Roberts. 2010. *Generation M²: Media in the Lives of 8- to 18-Year-Olds*. Menlo Park, CA: Henry J. Kaiser Family Foundation.

Rodesiler, Luke. 2022. *Bringing Sports Culture to the English Classroom: An Interest-Driven Approach to Literacy Instruction*. New York: Teachers College Press.

Scholastic. 2019. *Kids and Family Reading Report: Finding Their Story*. 7th ed. Scholastic (website). https://www.scholastic.com/content/dam/KFRR/Downloads/KFRReport_Finding%20Their%20Story.pdf.

Stallworth, B. Joyce, and Louel C. Gibbons. 2012. "What's on the List . . . Now? A Survey of Book-Length Works Taught in Secondary Schools." *English Leadership Quarterly* 34 (3): 2–3.

Tatum, Alfred. 2009. *Reading for Their Life: (Re)Building Textual Lineages of African American Males*. Portsmouth, NH: Heinemann.

Wilhelm, Jeffrey D. 1996. *"You Gotta BE the Book": Teaching Engaged and Reflective Reading with Adolescents*. New York: Teachers College Press.

Wilhelm, Jeffrey D., and Michael W. Smith with Sharon Fransen. 2014. *Reading Unbound: Why Kids Need to Read What They Want—and Why We Should Let Them*. New York: Scholastic.

Willingham, Daniel. 2017. *The Reading Mind: A Cognitive Approach to Understanding How the Mind Reads*. San Francisco: Jossey-Bass.

Yatvin, Joanne. 2000. "Minority View." In *Report of the National Reading Panel: Teaching Children to Read*, by National Reading Panel, 444–49. Washington, DC: National Institutes of Health.

A FINAL REFLECTION ON VETERAN'S DAY

Manning, Molly Guptill. 2014. *When Books Went to War: The Stories That Helped Us Win World War II*. Boston: Houghton Mifflin.

INDEX

C

D

E

F

G

H

I

J

K

L

N

O

P

S

T

U

V

W

Y

Credits, continued from copyright page

IMAGE CREDITS